# BIRD DIVINATION AMONG THE TIBETANS

(NOTES ON DOCUMENT PELLIOT No. 3530, WITH A STUDY OF TIBETAN PHONOLOGY OF THE NINTH CENTURY).

BY

BERTHOLD LAUFER.

*Et illud quidam etiam his notum, avium voces volatusque interrogare.*
TACITUS, *Germania* X.

Extrait du *T'oung-pao*, 2e Série, Vol. XV, No. 1, Mars 1914.

## Impressum

Bibliografische Information der Deutschen Nationalbibliothek: Die Deutsche Nationalbibliothek verzeichnet diese Publikation in der Deutschen Nationalbibliografie; detaillierte bibliografische Daten sind im Internet über http://dnb.d-nb.de abrufbar.



Coverbild: www.purestockx.com

Verlag:
VDM Verlag Dr. Müller Aktiengesellschaft & Co. KG
Dudweiler Landstr. 125 a, 66123 Saarbrücken, Deutschland
Telefon +49 681 9100-698, Telefax +49 681 9100-988, Email: info@vdm-verlag.de

Herstellung in Deutschland:
Schaltungsdienst Lange o.H.G., Zehrensdorfer Str. 11, D-12277 Berlin
Books on Demand GmbH, Gutenbergring 53, D-22848 Norderstedt

**ISBN: 978-3-8364-4031-8**

**weis**

s ist ein Reprint. Ein Buch also, dessen Vorlage ein meist sehr altes und tvolles Werk ist. An manchen Stellen mögen sich daher Spuren des Gebrauchs len oder kleine Beschädigungen. Auch ist eine leichte Unschärfe im Schrift-l bei alten Vorlagen normal.

VDM Verlag Dr. Müller

# Vorwort

Ein Großteil der Erkenntnisse, auf denen unsere Wissenschaften heute aufbauen, gründen im Forscherdrang des 19. Jahrhunderts. Dieser Drang, die Welt zu entdecken, zu erklären, zu vermessen und zu systematisieren, schien in jener Epoche ungeheuer stark gewesen zu sein, so dass kaum ein Mensch, dem Bildung wichtig war, der studiert hatte, der Ehrgeiz besaß, sich diesem Wettlauf um Wissen entziehen konnte. Und so entstand eine große Menge an grundlegenden Werken – häufig so einfach und plausibel geschrieben, dass es selbst für Laien spannend ist darin zu lesen. Noch heute.

An den Universitäten bildeten sich neue Disziplinen und Fächer heraus, wie etwa die Sozialwissenschaften, die Psychologie, die Psychiatrie. Zuweilen unter großen Widerständen, denn die traditionellen Wissenschaften wie Medizin oder Philosophie wehrten sich gegen diese wortwörtliche Auf-Fächerung ihres geistigen Bestandes. Die neue Wissenschaftsidee jedoch obsiegte: Wissenschaft als Forschung um des Forschens willen. Wissenschaft als Selbstzweck.

Was Medizin, Biologie, Chemie betraf, wurde die gesamte zelluläre, molekulare, atomare Basis der Welt in einer Spanne von hundert Jahren freigeschaufelt und der Enthusiasmus über jede weitere Entdeckung schien so groß zu sein, dass man sich unbedingt mitteilen wollte. Und so entstanden neben den Büchern auch allerlei gelehrte Gesellschaften und wissenschaftliche Vereinigungen. Institute auch, die noch heute existieren und die die Namen bedeutender Wissenschaftler von damals tragen.

Im post-aufgeklärten und napoleonisch-revolutionierten Deutschland begann so nach und nach eine breite Bildungselite das intellektuelle Leben zu bestimmen und verschaffte sich Weltgeltung. Die ersten Nobelpreise in Physik und Medizin gingen 1901 an die deutschen Forscher Röntgen und von Behring, ein Jahr später erhielt Hermann Emil Fischer den Nobelpreis für Chemie. Ferne Länder, etwa Japan, übernahmen große Teile des deutschen Rechtssystems. Gelesen wurde eben überall.

„Edition Classic“ will den Autoren des 19. und des beginnenden 20. Jahrhunderts ein neues Forum geben, indem sie ihre Bücher wieder auflegt. Darunter sind viele uns noch heute geläufige Namen, aber auch solche, die – zu Unrecht – in Vergessenheit geraten sind. Wert gelesen zu werden sind sie alle.

Esther von Krosigk, Herausgeberin

# BIRD DIVINATION AMONG THE TIBETANS

(NOTES ON DOCUMENT PELLIOT No. 3530, WITH A STUDY OF TIBETAN PHONOLOGY OF THE NINTH CENTURY).

BY

**BERTHOLD LAUFER.**

*Et illud quidam etiam his notum, avium voces volatusque interrogare.*
TACITUS, *Germania* X.

Extrait du *T'oung-pao*, 2e Série, Vol. XV, No. 1, Mars 1914.

# BIRD DIVINATION AMONG THE TIBETANS

## (NOTES ON DOCUMENT PELLIOT No. 3530, WITH A STUDY OF TIBETAN PHONOLOGY OF THE NINTH CENTURY).

BY

**BERTHOLD LAUFER.**

*Et illud quidam etiam his notum, avium voces volatusque interrogare.*
TACITUS, *Germania* X.

Among the Tibetan manuscripts discovered by M. Paul Pelliot there is a roll of strong paper (provisional number 3530 of the *Bibliothèque Nationale*) measuring $0.85 \times 0.31$ m and containing a table of divination. This document has recently been published and translated by M. J. BACOT. [1] This gentleman has furnished proof of possessing a good knowledge of Tibetan in a former publication, [2] in which he gives a most useful list of 710 abbreviations occurring in the cursive style of writing (*dbu-med*) of the Tibetans, from a manuscript obtained by him on his journeys in eastern Tibet. It is gratifying to note that the tradition gloriously inaugurated in France by Abel-Rémusat, Burnouf and Foucaux, and worthily continued by L. Feer and S. Lévi, reincarnates itself in a young and fresh representative of the Tibetan field, who has enough

1) *La table des présages signifiés par l'éclair.* Texte tibétain, publié et traduit.. (*Journal asiatique*, Mars-Avril, 1913, pp. 445—449, with one plate).

2) *L'écriture cursive tibétaine* (*ibid.*, Janvier-Février, 1912, pp. 1—78). M. BACOT is also the author of a pamphlet *L'art tibétain* (Châlon-sur-Saône, 1911), and of two interesting books of travel *Dans les marches tibétaines* (Paris, 1909) and *Le Tibet révolté* (Paris, 1912).

courage and initiative to attack original problems. It is likewise matter of congratulation to us that the wonderful discoveries of M. Pelliot will considerably enrich Tibetan research and reanimate with new life this wofully neglected science. The volumes of the ancient Kanjur edition discovered by him in the Cave of the Thousand Buddhas (*Ts'ien fu tung*) of Kan-su and dating at the latest from the tenth, and more probably even from the ninth century, together with many Tibetan book-rolls from the same place, [1]) are materials bound to signal a new departure in the study of Tibetan philology, hitherto depending exclusively on the recent prints of the last centuries. We therefore feel justified in looking forward with great expectations to the elaboration of these important sources. The text published by M. Bacot is the first Tibetan document of the *Mission Pelliot* made accessible to science, and there is every reason to be grateful for this early publication and the pioneer work conscientiously performed by M. Bacot. It is a document of great interest, both from a philological and a religious point of view. The merit of M. Bacot in the editing and rendering of this text is considerable. First of all, he has honorably accomplished the difficult task of transcribing the cursive form of the original into the standard character (*dbu-can*), and, as far as can be judged by one who has not had the opportunity of viewing the original, generally in a convincing manner; he has recognized also some of the archaic forms of spelling, and correctly identified them with their modern equivalents; and above all, aside from minor details, he has made a correct translation of the divination table proper.

There are, however, two points of prime importance on which my opinion differs from the one expressed by M. Bacot. These points are the interpretation of the meaning of the Table, and the

1) Compare P. Pelliot, *La mission Pelliot en Asie centrale*, pp. 25, 26 (*Annales de la société de géographie commerciale*, Fasc. 4, Hanoi, 1909) and *B. E. F. E. O.*, Vol. VIII, 1908, p. 507.

rendering of the introductory note prefacing the Table. In regard to the latter, M. BACOT is inclined to view it as a series of rebuses which seem to have the raven as their subject. He consequently takes every verse (the entire preface is composed of twenty-nine verses, each consisting of a dactyl and two trochees, — a metre peculiarly Tibetan and not based on any Sanskrit model) as a single unit; while in my opinion the verses are mutually connected, and their interrelation brings out a coherent account furnishing the explanation for the divination table. As indicated by the very title of his essay, M. BACOT regards the latter as a list of forebodings announced by lightning; and in column I of the Table worked up by him, we meet the translation *en cas d'éclair à l'est*, etc. The Tibetan equivalent for this rendering is *ṅan zer na*, which literally means, "if there is evil speaking." No authority, native or foreign, is known to me which would justify the translation of this phrase by anything like "flash of lightning;" it simply means "to utter bad words," which may augur misfortune; hence *ṅan*, as JÄSCHKE (*Dictionary*, p. 126) says, has the further meaning of "evil, imprecation." The phrase *ṅan smras* is rendered in the dictionary *Zla-bai od-snaṅ* (fol. 29b, Peking, 1838) into Mongol *maghu käläksän*. In the present case, the term *ṅan zer* refers to the unpleasant and unlucky sounds of the voice of the crow or raven, which indeed, as expressly stated in the prefatory note, is the subject of divination in this Table. Moreover, the preface leaves no doubt as to who the recipient of the offerings is. It is plainly told there in Verse 8 (4 in the numbering of M. BACOT): *gtor-ma ni bya-la gtor*, "the offering is made to the bird," and this bird certainly is the raven (*p'o-rog*) [1]) spoken of in Verse 1, again mentioned in Verse 17, their various tones being described in V. 25—29.

In this Table, it is, accordingly, the question only of the raven,

1) The differentiation of the Tibetan words for "raven" and "crow" is explained below, in the first note relating to the translation of the preface.

not of lightning; no word for lightning (*glog* or *t'og*) occurs either in the Table or in the preface.[1]) The fact that this interpretation

---

1) It must be said, in opposition to M. Bacot's explanation, also that neither the Tibetans nor the Indians seem to have offerings to lightning, nor do I know that good or bad predictions are inferred in Tibet from the manner in which a flash of lightning strikes. M. Bacot assures us that analogous tables for divination from lightning are still in use in Tibet and Mongolia. It would be interesting to see such a table referred to by M. Bacot. In India, lightnings were classified according to color, a yellow lightning pointing to rain, a white one to famine, etc. (A. Hillebrandt, *Ritual-Litteratur. Vedische Opfer und Zauber*, p. 184, Strassburg, 1897). M. Bloomfield (*The Atharvaveda*, p. 80, Strassburg, 1899) speaks of a "goddess lightning" who is conciliated by charms to cause her to spare the stores of grain; but then, again, he identifies the divine eagle with lightning. Among the Romans, the lightning-flash was a solicited portent of great significance, not, however, for the divination of the magistrates, but for certain priestly ceremonies of the augurs (Hastings, *Encyclopaedia of Religion*, Vol. IV, p. 823). — In regard to thunder, a series of omens regulated according to the quarters exists among the Mongols. P. S. Pallas (*Sammlungen historischer Nachrichten über die mongolischen Völkerschaften*, Vol. II, p. 318, St. Petersburg, 1801) has extracted the following from a Mongol book styled by him *Jerrien-Gassool*: "When in the spring it thunders in the south, this is a good sign for every kind of cattle. When it thunders straight from an easterly direction, this signifies an inundation threatening the crops. When it thunders from the north, this is a good sign for all creatures. When it thunders in the north-west, this means much slush and wet weather in the spring; and, moreover, many new and strange reports will be heard throughout the world. When it thunders from the west very early, a very dry spring will follow. When it thunders early in the south-west, this means unclean diseases to men. When it thunders early in the south-east, locusts will destroy the grass." In regard to auguries, Pallas states that the bird of augury among the Kalmuk is the whitish buzzard called *tsaghan chuldu*; when it flies to the right of a tramping Kalmuk, he takes it to be a happy omen, thanking it with bows; when, however, it flies to his left, he turns his eyes away and dreads a disaster. They say that the right wing of this bird is directed by a *Burchan* or good spirit; the left one by an aerial demon, and nobody dares shoot this bird. According to Pallas, the flight of the eagle, the raven, and other birds, has no significance among the Kalmuk. The white owl is much noted by them, and looked upon as a felicitous bird. — Abou Bekr Abdesselam Ben Choaïb (*La divination par le tonnerre d'après le manuscrit marocain intitulé Er-Ra'adiya, Revue d'ethnographie et de sociologie*, 1913, pp. 90—99) translates a Moroccan manuscript (date not given) treating of divination from thunder-peals, according to their occurrence in the twelve months of the year. Also the Malays draw omens from thunder (W. W. Skeat, *Malay Magic*, p. 561) and lightning (p. 665). — The field of Tibetan divination and astrology is a subject as wide as ungrateful and unpleasant for research. It has been slightly touched upon in the general books on Tibetan Buddhism by E. Schlagintweit and L. A. Waddell. Some special contributions are by A. Weber, *Ueber eine magische Gebetsformel aus Tibet* (*Sitzungsberichte der preussischen Akademie*, 1884, pp. 77—83, 1 plate), and Waddell, *Some Ancient Indian Charms*

is to the point, will be especially gleaned from the text of the *Kākajariti* given below. The first column of M. BACOT's Table finds its explanation in the last clause of this text, where it is said: "When an omen causing fear is observed, a strewing oblation must be offered to the crow" (*ajigs-pai rtags mtʿoṅ-na, bya-rog-la gtor-ma dbul-bar byao*), and the flesh of the frog is the most essential of these offerings. The crow does not receive offerings in each and every case when an oracle is desired from its sounds, but only when it emits disastrous notes pointing to some calamity, and the object of the offering is the prevention of the threatening disaster. It is therefore logical to find in the first column of our Table, headed "the method of offerings," and indicating the kind of offerings for the nine (out of the ten) points of the compass, the conditional restriction *ṅan zer na*, for example, "when in the east (the crow) should utter unlucky sounds, milk must be offered," etc. The crow is believed to fly up in one of the nine points of the compass, and exactly the same situation is described in the beginning of the *Kākajariti*.

Among the offerings (*gtor-ma*, Skr. *bali*) enumerated in our Table, there are two distinctly revealing Indian influence, — the white mustard (Tib. *yuṅs-kar*, Skr. *sarshapa*), and *guggula*, itself a Sanskrit word.[1]) The question must naturally be raised, Is this practice

---

*from the Tibetan* (*Journal Anthrop. Institute*, Vol. XXIV, 1895, pp. 41—44, 1 plate). The most common method of fortune-telling is practised by means of dice (*śo*) in connection with divinatory charts. Interesting remarks on this subject are found in the excellent works of STEWART CULIN, *Chinese Games with Dice and Dominoes* (*Report of U. S. Nat. Mus. for* 1893, p. 536, Washington, 1895), and *Chess and Playing-Cards* (*ibid.*, for 1896, pp. 821—822, Wash., 1898). Also this practice doubtless originates in India, and should be studied some day with reference to the Indian dice games and oracles (compare A. WEBER, *Ueber ein indisches Würfel-Orakel*, *Monatsberichte Berl. Ak.*, 1859; A. F. R. HOERNLE, *The Bower Manuscript*, pp. 209, 210, 214; J. E. SCHRÖTER, *Pāçakakevalī*, Ein indisches Würfelorakel, Borna, 1900; and chiefly H. LÜDERS, *Das Würfelspiel im alten Indien*, *Abhandl. der K. Ges. der Wiss. zu Göttingen*, Berlin, 1907). There are several Tibetan books treating especially of dice oracles (see also E. H. WALSH, *Tibetan Game of de sho*, *Proc. A. S. B.*, 1903, p. 129).

1) Also rice and flowers are Indian offerings, the same as occur likewise in Burma

of divination from the notes of a crow of indigenous Tibetan origin, or is it rather a loan received from India? The Tibetan Tanjur contains

---

among the offerings to the Nat (L. Vossion, *Nat-worship among the Burmese*, p. 4, reprint from *Journal American Folk-Lore*, 1891), and the whole series of offerings may confidently be stated to be derived from Indian practice. "After bathing, with hands circled by swaying bracelets, she herself gave to the birds an offering of curds and boiled rice placed in a silver cup; ... she greatly honored the directions of fortune-tellers; she frequented all the soothsayers learned in signs; she showed all respect to those who understood the omens of birds" (*The Kādambarī of Bāṇa* translated by Miss C. M. Ridding, p. 56, London, 1896). — M. Bacot accepts the rendering *bois d'aigle* for *guggula* (Tibetanized *gu-gul*) given in the Tibetan Dictionary of the French Missionaries. But this is not correct. *Guggula* or *guggulu* is not at all a wood but a gum resin obtained from a tree (*Boswellia serrata*, sometimes called the Indian Olibanum tree) and utilized as incense (W. Roxborough, *Flora Indica*, p. 365; G. Watt, *Dictionary of the Economic Products of India*, Vol. I, p. 515). In more recent times this name has been extended also to the produce of *Balsamodendron Mukul*, which became known to the Greeks under the name βδέλλα (thus in *Periplus*, ed. Fabricius, pp. 76, 78, 90), then Grecized βδέλλιον (first in Dioscorides, Latinized bdellium in Pliny, *Nat. Hist.* XII, 9, 19, ed. Mayhoff, Vol. II, p. 388; compare Lassen, *Indische Altertumskunde*, Vol. I, p. 290, and H. Bretzl, *Botanische Forschungen des Alexanderzuges*, pp. 282–4, Leipzig, 1903) and to the Arabs under the word *moql* مقل (L. Leclerc, *Traité des simples*, Vol. III, p. 331, Paris, 1883, and J. Löw, *Aramäische Pflanzennamen*, p. 359, Leipzig, 1881). The meaning 'bdellion' is exclusively given for *guggula* in the Sanskrit dictionaries of St. Petersburg; this, however, is not the original but merely a subsequent (and probably erroneous) application of the word, nor is the identity of *bdellion* with *guggula*, as established by J. Jolly (*Medicin*, p. 18, *Grundriss d. indo-ar. Phil.*), correct. Watt says advisedly, "Care must be taken not to confuse this gum resin (*guggula*) with the olibanum or frankincense of commerce, or with Mukul. The true Sanskrit name for this plant is most probably Sallaki.." The Sanskrit name which Watt has in mind is *çallakī* or *sillakī*, *Boswellia thurifera*, yielding frankincense which is called *silha* (Tib. *si-la*). The Greek words *bdella* and *bdellion* are derived from Hebrew *bdolah*, *bĕdolah*; but "what it was remains very doubtful" (Yule and Burnell, *Hobson-Jobson*, pp. 76, 886). Regarding the Chinese names of *guggula* see Pelliot, *T'oung Pao*, 1912, p. 480. In his study of the names of perfumes occurring in Chao Ju-kua, M. Pelliot (*ibid.*, p. 474) alludes to the *Mahāvyutpatti* as one of the sources to be utilized for such research; I may be allowed to point out that the Sanskrit and Tibetan list of the thirteen names of perfumes contained in that dictionary was published by me in *Zeitschrift für Ethnologie*, 1896, *Verhandlungen*, p. 397, in connection with the Tibetan text and translation of the *Dhūpayogaratnamālā*; this certainly was *une œuvre de jeunesse* on which I could now easily improve. The most important source for our purposes doubtless is the *Hiang p'u* 香譜 by Hung Ch'u 洪芻 of the Sung period, reprinted in *T'ang Sung ts'ung shu*. Bretschneider (*Bot. Sin.*, pt. I, No. 153) mentions a work of the same title, but from the hand of Ye T'ing-kuei 葉廷珪 of the Sung.

a small treatise under the title *Kākajariti* indicated by G. Huth. [1]) The Indian method of divining from the calls of the crow is briefly expounded therein, and for this reason a literal translation of it may first be given. It will be recognized that the thoughts of this text move on the same line as the *document Pelliot*, and it will furnish to us the foundation for some further remarks on the latter. In order to facilitate immediate comparison of the two texts, I have numbered, in the Table published by M. Bacot, the series of the first vertical column with the Roman figures I—XI, and the nine series yielded by the nine quarters with the Arabic figures 1—9, so that by the combination of the two any of the ninety squares of the Table may be readily found. The references to the squares of this Table, placed in parentheses in the following text, indicate thought identity or analogy in the two documents. [2])

## Translation of Kākajariti.

Tanjur, Section Sūtra (*mdo*), Vol. 123, Fol. 221 (edition of Narthang).

---

1) *Sitzungsberichte der preussischen Akademie*, 1895, p. 275. Huth refers to "Schiefner in Weber's Indische Streifen I 275," which I have never seen, and which is not accessible to me.

2) After my translation was made from the Narthang edition of the Tanjur, I found that A. Schiefner (*Ueber ein indisches Krähenorakel*, *Mélanges asiatiques*, Vol. IV, St. Petersburg, 1863, pp. 1—14) had already edited and translated the same work. In collating my rendering with that of Schiefner, it turned out that I differed from him in a number of points which are discussed in the footnotes. Schiefner's text (apparently based on the Palace edition) and translation are generally good, though the mark is missed in several passages; I have to express my acknowledgment especially to his text edition, as my copy of the Narthang print, which is difficult to read, left several points obscure. On the other hand, whoever will take the trouble to check my version with that of my predecessor, will doubtless recognize the independence of my work. As the principal point in the present case is to reveal the inward connection between the *Kākajariti* and the *document Pelliot*, it was, at any rate, necessary to place a complete version of that text before the reader, and not everybody may have access to the publication in which Schiefner's study is contained.

In Sanskrit: *Kākajariti* ("On the Sounds of the Crow"). [1])

In Tibetan: *Bya-rog-gi skad brtag-par bya-ba* ("Examination of the Sounds of the Crow").

This matter is as follows. The crows are divided into four castes; namely, Brāhmaṇa, Kshatriya, Vaiçya, and Çūdra. A crow of intelligent mind [2]) belongs to the Brāhmaṇa caste, a red-eyed

---

1) The Sanskrit title is thought by SCHIEFNER to be corrupt. He made two conjectures, — first, in a communication to Weber, by restoring the title into *kākarutaṁ*, which he soon rejected; second, he accepted as foundation of the disfigured Sanskrit title the words *bya-rog-gi spyod-pa* occurring at the end of the treatise, which he took in the sense of *kākacaritra* or *°carita*, and he assumed that this title may have arisen through a retranslation from Tibetan into Sanskrit, at a time when the Sanskrit original no longer existed. Again, on p. 14, he conjectures *spyod-pa* to be an error for *dpyod-pa* = Skr. *vicāraṇa*, "examination," and thus unconsciously contradicts his previous surmise on p. 1. I can see no valid reason for any of these conjectures. The final words taken for the title do not in fact represent it, but only refer to the third and last part of the treatise, which is plainly divided into three sections: 1. Omens obtained from a combination of orientation and the time divisions of the day; 2. Omens to be heeded by a traveller; 3. Omens obtained from the orientation of the crow's nest. The *spyod-pa* of the crows refers to the peculiar activity or behavior of the birds in building their nests. Besides, the title of the work is simply enough indicated in its Tibetan translation, "Examination of the Sounds (or Cries) of the Crow (or Crows)," and the restoration of the Sanskrit title should be attempted only on this basis. It is evident that it is defective, and that a word corresponding to Tib. *brtag-par bya-ba* is wanting, which, judging from analogies of titles in the Tanjur, it may be supposed, was *parīkshā*. The word *jarati*, corresponding to Tib. *skad*, seems to be a derivation from the root *jar*, *jarate*, "to call, to invoke."

2) Tib. *žo-la rtsi-ba*. SCHIEFNER (p. 12) remarks on this passage which he renders *die in Karsha's rechnenden Brahmanen*: "The Tibetan text is not quite without blemish. Some passages of the original are wholly misunderstood; to these belongs the passage in question. I suspect a misunderstanding of *kārshṇya*, 'blackness.' As Weber observes, this supposition is confirmed by a classification of the Brahmans among the crows occurring elsewhere." This interpretation seems to me to be rather artificial; I think *žo* is a clerical error for *že*, and take *že-la rtsi-ba* in the sense of "to calculate in their minds." The crow is the object of divinatory calculation on the part of observing man, and the bird which, owing to its superior intelligence, easily adapts itself to this process, is considered to rank among the highest caste. The ability for calculation and divination is directly transferred to the bird. The division into castes is found also among the Nāga and the spirits called *gňan* (see SCHIEFNER, *Ueber das Bonpo-Sūtra*, *Mém. Acad. de St. Pét.*, Vol. XXVIII, N°. 1, 1880, pp. 3, 26 *et passim*; *Mém. Soc. finno-ougrienne*, Vol. XI, 1898, p. 105; *Denkschriften Wiener Akademie*, Vol. XLVI, 1900, p. 31).

one to the Kshatriya caste, one flapping its wings to the Vaiçya caste, one shaped like a fish to the Çūdra caste, one subsisting on filthy food and craving for flesh belongs likewise to the latter.

The following holds good for the different kinds of tones emitted by the crow. The layman must pronounce the affair the truth of which he wishes to ascertain simultaneously [with the flight of the crow]. 1)

I. When in the first watch (*t'un dañ-po la*), 2) in the east, a crow sounds its notes, the wishes of men will be fulfilled.

When in the south-east it sounds its notes, an enemy will approach (Table II, 9, and V, 2). 3)

---

1) Schiefner translates: „Die verschiedenen Arten ihres Geschreis sind folgende, (welche) der Hausherr einmal wahrgenommen verkünden muss." But this mode of rendering the passage does not do justice to the text (*k'yim-bdag-gis cig-car bden-par ạgyur-ba ni brjod-par bya-ste*). Stress is laid on the phrase *cig-car*, alluding to the fact, which repeats itself in all systems of omens, that the wish must be uttered at the same moment when the phenomenon from which the oracle is taken occurs. Schiefner overlooks the force of *bden par ạgyur-ba*, which is not *wahrgenommen*, but *was bewahrheitet werden soll*. Only he who seeks an oracle will naturally pay attention to the flight of the crow, and he must loudly proclaim his question, addressing the bird at the moment when it flies into the open.

2) Schiefner takes the term *t'un* (Skr. *yāma*) in the sense of night-watch. This, in my opinion, is impossible. In this first section of the treatise, divination is detailed to five divisions of time, the fifth and last of which is designated as the sunset. Consequently the four preceding divisions must refer to the time of the day; both *t'un* and *yāma* apply to the day as well as to the night, and simply signify a certain length of time (usually identified with a period of three hours in our mode of reckoning) of the twenty-four hour day. The five watches named in our text would accordingly yield an average term of fifteen hours, the usual length of a day in India. It is also natural to watch crows in the daytime, and not at night, when, like others of their kind, they are asleep in their nests. The same division of the day into five parts, probably derived from India, exists also in Java (Raffles, *A History of Java*, Vol. I, p. 530, London, 1830).

3) The crow's prophecy of war is linked with the rapacious and bellicose character of the bird. This notion appears as early as in the Assyrian inscriptions of Sennacherib, where we meet such comparisons as "like the coming of many ravens swiftly moving over the country to do him harm," and "like an invasion of many ravens on the face of the country forcibly they came to make battle" (F. Delitzsch, *Assyrische Thiernamen*, p. 102, Leipzig, 1874; and W. Houghton, *The Birds of the Assyrian Monuments*, *Trans. Soc. Bibl. Arch.*, Vol. VIII, 1884, p. 80). In Teutonic divination, the raven believed to possess wisdom and knowledge of events was especially connected with battle: should one be heard thrice screaming on the roof, it boded death to warriors; while the appearance of ravens

When in the south, etc., a friend will visit (Table VIII, 6; X, 3).

When in the south-west, etc., unexpected profit will accrue.

When in the west, etc., a great wind will rise (Table V, 4).

When in the north-west, etc., a stranger (guest) will appear. [1])

When in the north, etc., property scattered here and there (*nor gtor-ba*) will be found (Table X, 2).

When in the north-east, etc., a woman will come (Table VII, 8; IX, 5).

When in the abode of Brahma (zenith), [2]) etc., a demon will

---

following a host or a single warrior would bring good luck in battle (HASTINGS, *Encyclopaedia of Religion*, Vol. IV, p. 827).

1) In southern India, if a crow keeps on cawing incessantly in a house, it is believed to foretell the coming of a guest. The belief is so strong, that some women prepare more food than is required for the household (E. THURSTON, *Ethnographic Notes in Southern India*, p. 276, Madras, 1906). Among the Pārsī (J. J. MODI, *Omens among the Parsees*, in his *Anthropological Papers*, p. 4, Bombay, no year) the cawing of a crow portends good as well as evil. A peculiar sound called "a full noise" portends good. Such a noise is also considered to foretell the arrival of a guest or the receipt of a letter from a relative in some distant country. If a good event occurs after the peculiar cawing which portends good, they present some sweets to a crow. Another peculiar kind of cawing, especially that of the *kāgri*, the female crow, portends some evil. A crow making such a peculiar noise is generally driven away with the remark, "Go away, bring some good news!"

2) The four cardinal points (*p'yogs bži*) are expressed by the common words *šar*, *lho*, *nub*, *byaṅ*. The four intermediate points are designated *me* ("fire"), south-east; *bden bral*, south-west; *rluṅ* ("wind"), north-west; and *dbaṅ-ldan*, north-east. These names are derived from those of the Ten Guardians of the World (see *Mahāvyutpatti*, ed. of MINAYEV and MIRONOV, p. 102; ed. of CSOMA and ROSS, pt. 1, p. 57). The ninth point, Brāhmī, is there rendered by *steṅ-gi p'yogs*, the direction above, which is expressed in our text by *Ts'aṅs-pai gnas*, the place of Brahma. In the Table published by M. BACOT (II, 9) the term *nam-ka* (= *k'a*, *mk'a*) *ldiṅ* is used in lieu of that one; this means literally "floating or soaring in the sky" (it occurs as a frequent name of the Garuḍa), and here "soaring in straight direction toward the sky," that is, the zenith. It will thus be seen that the nine points of the compass (out of the typical ten, *daçadik*, which were assumed), as enumerated in the above text, are the same and occur in the same succession, as in M. BACOT's Table. The tenth point, naturally, is here out of the question, as crows cannot fly up in the nadir of a person. In the introductory to M. Pelliot's roll the fact of nine cardinal points is distinctly alluded to in two verses (6 and 24), and M. BACOT, quite correctly, has recognized there the eight quarters, making nine with the zenith. — The connection of crow auguries with the cardinal points may have arisen from the very ancient observation

come (Table X, 1).[1])

End of the cycle of the first watch.

II. When in the second watch (*t'un gñis-pa-la*), in the east, a crow sounds its notes, near relatives will come (Table VI, 4).[2])

---

of the crow's sense of locality, and its utilization in discovering land. Indian navigators kept birds on board ship for the purpose of despatching them in search of land. In the *Bāveru-Jātaka* (No. 339 of the series) it is a crow, in the *Kevaddhasutta* (in *Dīghanikāya*) it is a "land-spying bird." J. MINAYEV (*Mélanges asiatiques*, Vol. VI, 1872, p. 597), who was the first to edit the former text, explained the word for the crow *disākāka*, as it occurs there, as possibly meaning "a crow serving to direct navigators in the four quarters" (while the opinion of WEBER, added by him, that it might be an ordinary crow, as it occurs in all quarters, — seems forced). In my opinion, MINAYEV is correct: *disākāka* is the crow, whose flight is affiliated with the quarters, both in navigation and divination. GRÜNWEDEL (*Veröff. Mus. für Völkerkunde*, Vol. V, 1897, p. 105) has published an allied text from the Biography of Padmasambhava, where the land-seeking bird of the navigators is designated "pigeon" (Tib. *p'ug-ron*). This will doubtless go back to some unknown Indian text where pigeons are mentioned in this capacity. PLINY (*Nat. Hist.* VI, 22, 83, ed. MAYHOFF, Vol. I, p. 465) relates that the seafarers of Taprobane (Ceylon) did not observe the stars for the purpose of navigation, but carried birds out to sea, which they sent off from time to time, and then followed the course of the birds flying in the direction of the land (siderum in navigando nulla observatio: septentrio non cernitur, volucres secum vehunt emittentes saepius meatumque earum terram petentium comitantur). The connection of this practice with that described in the Babylonian and Hebrew traditions of the Deluge was long ago recognized. In the Babylonian record (H. ZIMMERN, *Keilinschriften und Bibel*, p. 7) a pigeon, a swallow, and a raven are sent out successively to ascertain how far the waters have abated. When the people of Thera emigrated to Libya, ravens flew along with them ahead of the ships to show the way. The Viking, sailing from Norway in the ninth century, maintained birds on board, which were set free in the open sea from time to time, and discovered Iceland with their assistance (O. KELLER, *Die antike Tierwelt*, Vol. II, p. 102). According to JUSTIN (XXIV. IV. 4), who says that the Celts were skilled beyond other peoples in the science of augury, it was by the flight of birds that the Gauls who invaded Illyricum were guided (DOTTIN in HASTINGS, *Encyclopaedia of Religion*, Vol. IV, p. 787). In the *Ise-fūdoki*, Emperor Jimmu engaged in a war expedition, and marched under the guidance of the gold-colored raven (K. FLORENZ, *Japanische Mythologie*, p. 299). On the sending of pheasant and raven in ancient Japan see especially A. PFIZMAIER, *Zu der Sage von Owo-kuni-nushi* (*Sitzungsberichte Wiener Akademie*, Vol. LIV, 1866, pp. 50—52).

1) SCHIEFNER reads *agron-po*, and accordingly translates "guest." But it seems unlikely that the same should be repeated here that was said a few lines before in regard to the north-west. The Narthang print plainly has *agon-po*, which I think is mistaken for *agoṅ-po*, "demon." The analogous case in Table X, 1, where the word *adre gdon* is used, confirms this supposition.

2) In the Kanjur, a little story is told of a crow uttering agreeable sounds auguring

[A reference in regard to the south-east is lacking in the text.]

When in the south it sounds its notes, you will obtain flowers and areca-nuts. [1])

When in the south-west, etc., there will be numerous offspring (*rgyud-pa ạp'el-bar ạgyur-ro*).

When in the west, etc., you will have to set out on a distant journey (*t'ag riṅs-su ạgro-bar ạgyur-ro*; compare Table II, 2; IX, 3).

When in the north-west, etc., this is a prognostic of the king being replaced by another one (*rgyal-po gžan-du ạgyur-bai rtags*; compare Table VIII, 1). [2])

When in the north, etc., you will receive good news to hear (Table III, 8; VII, 7). [3])

---

for the safe return of a woman's absent husband, and being rewarded by her with a golden cap (A. SCHIEFNER, *Tibetan Tales*, English ed. by RALSTON, p. 355). J. J. MODI (*Anthropological Papers*, p. 28) quotes the following lines, which he overheard a Hindu woman speak to a crow: "Oh crow, oh crow! (I will give thee) golden rings on thy feet, a ball prepared of curd and rice, a piece of silken cloth to cover thy loins, and pickles in thy mouth." A peculiar noise made by a crow, continues this author, is supposed to indicate the arrival of a dear relation or at least of a letter from him. When they hear a crow make that peculiar noise, they promise it all the above good things if its prediction turn out true. In this case they fulfill their promise by serving it some sweets, but withhold the ornaments and clothes. — The following custom is observed in Cambodja. "Lorsque quelqu'un de la maison est en pays lointain, si le corbeau vient gazouiller dans le voisinage, la face tournée dans la direction de l'absent, il annonce son prompt retour. Dans toute autre direction, il annonce un malheur" (É. AYMONIER, *Revue indochinoise*, 1883, p. 148).

1) Tib. *me-tog daṅ go-la t'ob-pa*. SCHIEFNER renders *go-la* by "betel;" but *go-la* is the areca-nut, which is chewed together with the leaf of betel, *piper betel* L. (see CHANDRA DAS, *Dictionary*, p. 227). We may justly raise the question whether anything so insipid was contained in the Sanskrit original, and whether the text is not rather corrupted here. The Table contains nothing to this effect. I venture to think that *go*, "rank, position," was intended. In Table I, 6, flowers are mentioned as offerings to the birds, and this may give a clew as to how the confusion came about.

2) In the text of the Table: *rgyal-po ạjig-par ston*, "this indicates the overthrow or ruin of the king" (but not *indique un danger pour le roi*). I do not agree with SCHIEFNER's rendering: „Ein Zeichen, dass der König sich anderswohin wendet."

3) Tib. *ạp'rin-las legs-par t'os-par ạgyur-ro*. *P'rin*, "news," will probably be the proper reading. In the text of M. BACOT *p'rin byaṅ* is printed, and translated *un courrier de nouvelles*. M. BACOT presumably had in mind the word *bya-ma-rta*, "a courier," but there is no word *byaṅ* with this meaning. We doubtless have to read *p'rin bzaṅ*, "good news, good message."

When in the north-east, etc., disorder [1]) will break out (Table V, 7).

When in the zenith, etc., you will obtain the fulfilment of your wishes. [2])

End of the cycle of the second watch.

III. When in the third watch, in the east, a crow sounds its notes, you will obtain property (Table X, 2).

When in the south-east a crow sounds its notes, a battle (*ạtˁab-mo*) will arise (Table V, 7).

When in the south, etc., a storm will come (Table V, 4).

When in the south-west, etc., an enemy will come (see above, I, south-east).

When in the west, etc., a woman will come (see above, I, north-east).

When in the north-west, etc., a relative will come (see above, II, east).

When in the north, etc., a good friend will come (Table VIII, 6; X, 3).

When in the north-east, etc., a conflagration will break out (*mes ạtsˁig-par ạgyur-ro*; Table VI, 7).

When in the zenith, etc., you will gain profit from being taken care of by the king. [3])

End of the cycle of the third watch.

---

1) Tib. *ạk'rug-pa* exactly corresponds in its various shades of meaning to Chinese *luan* 亂, "disorder, tumult, insurrections, war," etc. This rendering is indeed given for the Tibetan word in the Tibetan-Chinese vocabulary of *Hua i yi yü* (Ch. 11, p. 33 b; Hirth's copy in Royal Library of Berlin). In the Table, the word *t'ab-mo*, "fight, battle," is used.

2) Tib. *ạdod-pai ạjug-pa rñed-par ạgyur-ro*. SCHIEFNER translates: „Wird sich die gewünschte Gelegenheit finden."

3) SCHIEFNER's translation „wird der König den im Gemüth befestigten Gewinn finden" is unintelligible. The text reads: *rgyal-po t'ugs-la brtags-pai rñed-pa t'ob-par ạgyur-ro*. Schiefner's correction of *brtags* into *btags* is perfectly justifiable; indeed, the confusion of these two words is frequent. But *tˁugs-la ạdogs-pa* is a common phrase correctly explained by JÄSCHKE (*Dictionary*, p. 280) "to interest one's self in, to take care of." It should not be forgotten, of course, that, at the time when Schiefner wrote, this dictionary was not published.

IV. When in the fourth watch, in the east, a crow sounds its notes, it is a prognostic of great fear (*ajigs-pa cᶜe-bai rtags-so*; Table V, 6; IX, 1).

When in the south-east a crow sounds its notes, it is a prognostic of large gain.

When in the south, etc., a stranger (guest) will come (see above, I, north-west).

When in the south-west, etc., a storm will rise in seven days.

When in the west, etc., rain and wind will come (Table V, 4, 5). [1]

When in the north-west, etc., you will find property which is scattered here and there (*nor gtor-ba*).

When in the north, etc., a king will appear.

When in the north-east, etc., you will obtain rank. [2]

When in the zenith, etc., it is a prognostic of hunger.

End of the cycle of the three watches and a half.

V. When at the time of sunset (*ñi-ma nub-pai tsᶜe*; compare Table X), in the east, a crow sounds its notes, an enemy will appear on the road.

When in the south-east a crow sounds its notes, a treasure will come to you.

When in the south, etc., you will die of a disease (Table V, 8). [3]

---

1) The ability attributed to crow and raven of possessing a foreknowledge of coming rain has chiefly made them proëminently prophetic birds (*augur aquae* in Horace). The ancients observed that these birds used to caw with peculiar notes when rain was to fall, and that, if a storm was imminent, they were running to and fro on the beach with great restlessness, and bathing their heads (compare O. Keller, *Die antike Tierwelt*, Vol. II, p. 98).

2) Tib. *go-la* (as above) *rñed-par agyur-ro*. The correction *go rñed-par* may here be allowed to pass, as the finding of areca-nuts seems such a gross stupidity.

3) In the story "The Death of the Magpie," translated from a manuscript of the India Office by A. Schiefner (*Mélanges asiatiques*, Vol. VIII, p. 680), the raven has the attributes "the Uncle, the Judge of the Dead" (in Schiefner's rendering; the original is not known to me), and the following verses are addressed to it (p. 631): "Be kind to the nephews here, bestow fortune upon the children, direct the government of the country,

When in the south-west, [1] etc., the wishes of one's heart will be fulfilled.

When in the west, etc., relatives will come.

When in the north-west, etc., it is a prognostic of obtaining property.

When in the north, etc., homage will be done to the king.

[A reference to the north-east is lacking in the text.]

When in the zenith, etc., you will obtain an advantage for which you had hoped.

End of the cycle of the fourth watch.

End of the description of such-like cries of the crow.

We shall now discuss the import of the crow's tones when one is travelling. When along dams and river-banks, on a tree, in a ravine, [2] or on cross-roads, a crow sounds its voice on your right-hand side, you may know that this journey is good. When, at the time of wandering on the road, a crow sounds its voice behind your back, you will obtain the *siddhi*. When, during a journey, a crow flapping its wings [3] sounds its voice, a great acci-

---

lend expression to good plans." In connection with these ideas of the raven as a bird of death, it is worthy of note that in two texts of the Tanjur, Mahākāla appears in the form of the Raven-faced one (Skr. *kākāsya*, Tib. *bya-rog gdoṅ-can*), likewise the goddess Kālī (Tib. *k'va gdoṅ-ma*); see P. Cordier, *Cat. du fonds tibétain de la Bibl. Nat.*, Vol. II, pp. 124, 127. The raven-faced Mahākāla is illustrated in the "Three Hundred Gods of Narthang" (section *Rin ąbyuṅ*, fol. 121). The raven as a bird announcing death is widely known in classical antiquity and mediæval Europe (O. Keller, *Die antike Tierwelt*, Vol. II, p. 97; E. A. Poe's poem *The Raven*). The imminent deaths of Tiberius, Gracchus, Cicero, and Sejan, were prophesied by ravens.

1) Is expressed in this passage by *srin-poi mts'ams*, "the intermediate space of the Rākshasa."

2) Tib. *grog stod*, as plainly written in the Narthang print. Schiefner read *grog stoṅ*, and corrected *grog steṅ*, with the translation "on an ant-heap," regarding *grog* as *grog-ma*, *grog-mo*, "ant." I prefer to conceive *grog* as *grog-po* (related to *roṅ*), "ravine," which is more plausible in view of the other designations of localities which are here grouped together. Moreover, I do not believe that crows go near ant-hills or feed on ants. The reading *stod* is then perfectly good, the significance being "in the upper part of the ravine."

3) According to the introduction, one of the Kshatriya caste.

dent will befall one. When, during a journey, a crow pulling human hair with its beak [1]) sounds its voice, it is an omen that one will die at that time. When, during a journey, a crow eating filthy food [2]) sounds its voice, it is an omen of food and drink being about to come (Table VIII, 9).

When, during a journey, a crow perching on a thorn-bush sounds its voice, it should be known that there is occasion to fear an enemy. When, during a journey, a crow perching on a tree with milky sap [3]) sounds its voice, milk-rice (*o tʻug-gi bza-ba*) will fall to your lot at that time. When a crow perching on a withered tree [4]) sounds its voice, it is a prognostication of the lack of food and drink at that time. When a crow perching on a palace sounds its voice, you will find an excellent halting-place. [5]) When a crow

---

1) Tib. *skra mcʻus gziṅs-šiṅ*. According to Jäschke (*Dictionary*, p. 464) *skra ądsiṅs-pa* or *gziṅ-ba* is an adjective with the meaning "bristly, rugged, shaggy" (*Dictionary of the French Missionaries*, p. 832: *crines disjecti, cheveux épars*). The verbal particle *ciṅ* and the instrumentalis *mcʻu-s* ("with the beak") indicate that *gziṅs* is a verbal form belonging to a stem *dziṅs*, *ądziṅs*, and means "pulling about hair in such a way that it appears rugged." Below, we find the same expression *mcʻus gos gziṅs-šiṅ*, "pulling a dress with its beak." The word *ądsiṅs-pa* is used also of interlaced trees or thick-set vegetation, as indicated by the Polyglot Dictionary of Kʻien-lung, according to which it is the equivalent of *tsʻao mu tsʻung tsa* 草木叢雜, Manchu *gubulehebi*, Mongol *küghänäldüji* (*s'entrelacer*); we find there, further, the phrase *sgro ądziṅs* = *ling chʻi tsʻan küe* 翎翅殘缺, "with broken wings," Mongol *sämtäräji*, *se briser* (the Tibetan equivalent in Kovalevski is a misprint). Schiefner (p. 14) remarks that the form *gziṅs* is new to him, and questions its correctness; he takes it as identical with *bzuṅ*, and translates it by *anfassen*. This derivation is not correct, it is merely surmised. The passage evidently means more than that the crow simply seizes human hair; it is torn to pieces, and this destructive work has a distinct relation to the foreboding of death.

2) Tib. *mi gtsaṅ-ba za žiṅ*, the same expression as used in the introduction to denote a crow of the Çūdra caste. Compare *Subhāshitaratnanidhi* 37 (ed. Csoma).

3) Tib. *o-ma-can-gyi šiṅ* (Skr. *kshīrikā*, *kshīriṇī*). Indian medicine recognizes five trees presumed to yield a milky sap. These are, according to Hoernle (*The Bower Manuscript*, p. 20), the nyagrodha (*Ficus bengalensis*), udumbara (*Ficus glomerata*), açvattha (*Ficus religiosa*), plaksha (*Ficus tjakela*), and pārīsha (*Thespesia populnea*).

4) As often in the Indian stories (Schiefner, *Mélanges asiatiques*, Vol. VIII, 1877, p. 96; or Ralston, Tibetan Tales, p. 32).

5) Schiefner translates erroneously, "When you betook yourself to the royal palace,

perching on a divan sounds its note, an enemy will come. When a crow facing the door sounds its voice, it should be known that a peril will threaten from the frontier (*mts'ams-kyi ajigs-par šes-par byao*). When a crow pulling a dress (*gos*) with its beak sounds its voice, you will find a dress (*gos*). When, during a journey, a crow perching on the cranium of a corpse [1]) sounds its notes, it is a prognostication of death. When a crow seizing a red thread and perching on the roof of a house sounds its notes, this house will be destroyed by fire (Table VI, 7). When, in the morning (*sña-droi dus-su,* Table V), many crows assemble, a great storm will arise (Table V, 3). [2])

When, at the time of a journey, a crow seizing with its beak a piece of wood sounds its voice, some advantage will fall to your lot. When, at the time of a journey, at sunrise (*ñi-ma šar dus-su,* Table IV), a crow sounds its voice, you will obtain property. When, at the time of a journey, it sounds its voice, [3]) one's wishes will be fulfilled.

---

and when the crow then sounds its cries, you will receive a good seat." But it is the question of a traveller who, on his journey, happens to pass by a palace, and it is the crow which is sitting on the roof of the palace (the verb *gnas* means "to dwell, remain," but never expresses any act of motion); in the same manner as the crow has found a good resting-place, so the weary wanderer will find good quarters for the night. The text runs thus: *p'o-brañ-la gnas-nas gañ-gi ts'e skad sgrogs-na, dei ts'e sdod sa bzañ-po rñed-par agyur-ro.* The word *sdod sa* does not mean "a seat," but a place where a traveller stops for the night, "halting-place." Likewise, in the two following sentences, SCHIEFNER refers the phrases *gdan-la gnas-nas* and *sgo lta žiñ* to the man instead of to the crow.

1) SCHIEFNER: „eine Krähe auf der Kopfbinde sich befindend." This is due to a confusion of the two words *t'od* and *t'od-pa*; the former means "turban;" but the text has *t'od-pa* meaning "the skull of a dead person," and this only makes sense of the passage. Crows congregate and feed on carrion, and are therefore conceived of as birds of death. The turban, for the rest, is out of the question in this text, as it was introduced into India only by the Mohammedans.

2) O. KELLER (*Die antike Tierwelt,* Vol. II, p. 109, Leipzig, 1913), who concludes his interesting chapter on crow and raven in classical antiquity with an extract from Schiefner's translation, observes on this sentence that it is based on a fact, and that such grains of truth hidden among these superstitions account for the fact that they could survive for centuries.

3) Apparently there is here a gap in the text, no definition of the activity of the crow being given.

End of the signs of the journey (*lam-gyi mtsʿan-ñid*).

The symptoms (or omens) of the nest-building of the crow are as follows. [1] When a crow has built its nest in a branch on the east side of a tree, a good year and rain will then be the result of it. When it has built its nest on a southern branch, the crops will then be bad. When it has built its nest on a branch in the middle of a tree, a great fright will then be the result of it (Table V, 6). When it makes its nest below, fear of the army of one's adversary will be the result of it. When it makes its nest on a wall, on the ground, or on a river, the king will be healed [from a disease]. [2]

Further, the following explanation is to be noted. When a crow sounds the tone *ka-ka*, you will obtain property. When a crow sounds the tone *da-da*, misery will befall you. When a crow sounds the tone *ta-ta*, you will find a dress. When a crow sounds the tone *gha-gha*, a state of happiness will be attained. [3] When a crow sounds the tone *gha-ga*, a failure will be the result of it. [4]

---

1) In the first section of the treatise the crow is in motion, and the person demanding the oracle is stationary. In the second section both the crow and the person are in motion. In this one, the third section, both the crow and the person are stationary; hence the text says: *gnas-pai bya-rog-gi tsʿañ-gi mtsʿan-ñid*, "the crows when they are settled..."

2) Tib. *ạtsʿo-bar ạgyur-ro*, translated by SCHIEFNER „so wird der König leben," which gives no sense. Of course, the word *ạtsʿo-ba* means "to live," but also "to recover from sickness." Here the Table (IX, 2) comes to our rescue, where we meet the plain wording *nad-pa sos-par ston*, "it indicates cure from disease." — Among the Greeks, the crow, owing to the belief in the long life of the bird, was an emblem of Asklepios (O. KELLER, *Die antike Tierwelt*, Vol. II, p. 105); compare Hesiod's famous riddle on the age of the crow and raven (W. SCHULTZ, *Rätsel aus dem hellenischen Kulturkreise*, p. 143, Leipzig, 1912; and K. OHLERT, *Rätsel und Rätselspiele der alten Griechen*, 2d ed., p. 146, Berlin, 1912). The idea of the longevity of the crow was entertained also in India (Skr. *dīrghāyus*, Tib. *na-tsʿod-can*, attribute of the crow given in the *Dictionary of the French Missionaries*, p. 86); it is striking that this quality of the crow is not alluded to in our text.

3) Tib. *don ạgrub-par ạgyur-ro.* SCHIEFNER translates: „so geht die Sache in Erfüllung."

4) Tib. *nor oñ-bar ạgyur-ro.* SCHIEFNER, „so wird ein Schatz kommen," which is certainly correct, as far as the meaning of these words is concerned; but I doubt very much whether this is the true significance intended by the author, for what SCHIEFNER trans-

When an omen causing fear is observed, a strewing oblation must be offered to the crow. As the flesh of a frog pleases the crow, no accidents will occur when frog-flesh is offered. [1])

*Oṁ mi-ri mi-ri vajra tudaṭe gilaṁ gṛihṇa gi svāhā!*

End of the description of such-like behavior of the crow.

Translated by the Mahāpaṇḍita Dānaçīla in the monastery T'aṅ-po-c'e of Yar-kluṅs in the province of dBus.

---

The translator Dānaçīla has been dated by Huth in the ninth century, on the ground that he is made a contemporary of King K'ri-lde sroṅ-btsan of Tibet in the work *sGra sbyor* in Tanjur, Sūtra, Vol. 124. This fact is correct, as may be vouchsafed from a copy made by me of this work. Dānaçīla figures there, together with such well-known names as Jinamitra, Surendrabodhi, Çrīlendrabodhi, Bodhimitra, the Tibetan Ratnarakshita, Dharmatāçīla, Jñānasena, Jayarakshita, Mañjuçrīvarma and Ratnendraçīla. Dānaçīla is well known as translator of many works in the Kanjur [2]) and Tanjur. From the colophon of a work in the latter collection it appears that he hailed from Varendrajīgatāla, that is, Jīgatāla

lates is exactly the same as what is said above in regard to the tone *ka-ka*. Further, the tone *gha-ga* stands in opposition to the preceding tone *gha-gha*; it thus becomes clear that *nor* stands for *nor-ba*, "to err, to fail," and is expressive of the contrary of *don ągrub-pa*, "to reach one's aim, to obtain one's end, to attain to happiness." This case reminds one of the grammatical as well as other subtleties of the Indian mind. — Also the ancients seem to have distinguished between various kinds of raven's cries, judging from Pliny's words that they imply the worst omen when the birds swallow their voice, as if they were being choked (pessima eorum significatio, cum gluttiunt vocem velut strangulati. *Nat. Hist.*, X, 12, § 32; ed. Mayhoff, Vol. II, p. 229). The crow, according to Pliny (*ibid.*, § 30), is a bird inauspicatae garrulitatis, a quibusdam tamen laudata.

1) In the belief of the Tibetans, the crow is fond of frogs; compare the jolly story "The Frog and the Crow" in W. F. O'Connor, *Folk Tales from Tibet*, p. 48 (London, 1906).

2) Feer, *Annales du Musée Guimet*, Vol. II, p. 406.

(Jagaddala) in Varendra, in eastern India. [1] Then we meet him in Kaçmīra, where Tāranātha [2] knows him together with Jinamitra and Sarvajñadeva, in accordance with *dPag bsam ljon bzaṅ* (ed. Chandra Das, p. 115); while *rGyal rabs* has the triad Jinamitra, Çrīlendrabodhi, and Dānaçīla. [3] It may therefore be granted that the *Kākajariti* [4] was translated and known in Tibet in the first part of the ninth century. The original Sanskrit manuscript from which the Tibetan translation was made in all probability was defective, for three gaps in it could unmistakably be pointed out.

What is the position of *K.* in the history of Indian divination? H. Jacobi (in Hastings, *Encyclopaedia of Religion*, Vol. IV, p. 799) has formulated the result of his study of this subject in these words: "In India, divination has gone through two phases of development. Originally it seems to have been practised chiefly with the intention of obviating the evil consequences of omens and portents; in the later period, rather to ascertain the exact nature of the good or evil which those signs were supposed to indicate." In the Vedic Saṁhitās, birds are invoked to be auspicious, and certain birds, especially pigeons or owls, are said to be messengers

1) P. Cordier, *Cat. du fonds tibétain de la Bibl. Nat.* II, pp. 63, 122, 188 (Paris, 1909), and Vidyabhusana (the name of this author appears in his publications in four different ways of spelling, ₒbhusan, ₒbhusana, ₒbhuṣana, ₒbhuṣaṇa: which is the bibliographer supposed to choose?) ‚*Bauddha-Stotra-Saṁgrahaḥ*, pp. XVIII, XIX (Calcutta, 1908). Mr. V. states that it is said at the end of the *Ekajaṭīsādhana* that the worship of Tārā originated from China, but that it is not clear whether this refers to Ekajaṭī Tārā alone or to Tārā of all classes. I fear that neither the one nor the other is the case. The Tibetan text plainly says, "The work *Tārāsādhana* which has come from China (*scil.* in a Chinese translation) is in a perfect condition." This implies that the Tibetan translator availed himself of a Chinese version. The worship of Tārā most assuredly originated in India, not in China.

2) Schiefner's translation, p. 226.

3) Schlagintweit, Könige von Tibet, p. 849; also Rockhill, *The Life of the Buddha*, p. 224.

4) Henceforth abbreviated *K.*

of death (Nirṛti, Yama). [1]) But all these are no more than scant

1) The best investigation of the history of bird omens in India is found in the monograph of E. HULTZSCH (*Prolegomena zu des Vasantarāja Çākuna nebst Textproben*, Leipzig, 1879). The beginnings of bird augury in India may be traced back to the Vedic period. In the Ṛigveda occur the so-called *çākuna*, charms against pigeons, owls, and other black birds whose appearance or contact forebodes evil, or defiles (M. BLOOMFIELD, *The Atharva-veda*, p. 85, Strassburg, 1899). According to MACDONELL and KEITH (*Vedic Index of Names and Subjects*, Vol. II, p. 347, London, 1912) there are the two words, *çakuna*, usually denoting a large bird, or a bird which gives omens, and *çakuni*, used practically like the former, but with a much clearer reference to divination, giving signs and fore-telling ill-luck; later the falcon is so called, but the raven may be intended; the commentator on the *Taittirīya Saṃhitā* thinks that it is the crow. Oracles obtained from an observation of crows seem to be contained particularly in the *Kauçika Sūtra*. When the rite serving the purpose of securing a husband has been performed on behalf of a girl, the suitor is supposed to appear from the direction from which the crows come (H. OLDENBERG, *Die Religion des Veda*, p. 511, Berlin, 1894). Contact with a crow was regarded as unlucky and defiling. He who was touched by a crow was thrice turned around himself, from the left to the right. by the sorcerer holding a burning torch (V. HENRY, *La magie dans l'Inde antique*, p. 176, 2d ed., Paris, 1909; E. THURSTON, *Ethnographic Notes in Southern India*, p. 277, Madras, 1906). A. HILLEBRANDT (*Ritual-Litteratur. Vedische Opfer und Zauber*, p. 183, Strassburg, 1897) believes he finds the explanation for this idea of bird omens in a passage of Baudhāyana, according to which the birds are the likenesses of the manes; but it seems rather doubtful whether the latter notion could receive such a generalized interpretation, and whether it is sufficient to account for the augural practice in its entire range. The latter would naturally presuppose the idea of the bird being animated with a soul and being gifted with supernatural powers or instigated by some divine force; but Hillebrandt's opinion leaves the reason unexplained why the bird, even though it should represent a mane in every case, possesses the ability of divination. True it is, as shown by W. CALAND (*Die altindischen Todten- und Bestattungsgebräuche*, p. 78, Amsterdam, 1896), that especially the crows were conceived of as embodying the souls of the departed, as messengers of Yama, who, after the funerary repast (*çrāddha*), draw near, greedy for food (compare the Raven Spirit in the Lamaist mystery plays who attempts to filch the strewing oblation, and who is chased away by two stick-brandishing Atsara, the skeleton ghosts!); but plainly, in this case, no process of divination is in question. CALAND, on this occasion, quotes DUBOIS on the modern practice that the chief of the funeral offers boiled rice and pease to the crows, — if they should refuse to eat, it is taken as an evil presage of the future state of the deceased; but this evidently is quite a different affair from that described in his above reference to Baudhāyana. Some authors allow the whole practice of auguries to go back into the prehistoric epoch of the Indo-European peoples (H. HIRT, *Die Indogermanen*, Vol. II, p. 518, Strassburg, 1907; and S. FEIST, *Kultur*, etc., *der Indogermanen*, p. 326, Berlin, 1913), the latter even going so far as to speculate that the idea of a soul flying along in the shape of a bird was not foreign to the *urvolk*, since this augural divination is based on the transformation of the souls into birds. I am very skeptical regarding such conclusions and constructions, and must confess that

allusions; neither in the Vedic nor in the early Brahmanic epoch do we find anything like an elaborate augural system, as in *K.*, in which future events are predicted, — Jacobi's second stage. The same author tells us that the whole art of divination became independent of religion when Greek astronomy and astrology were introduced into India in the early centuries of our era; the Indian astrologer then took up divination, hitherto practised by the Atharva priest. It is of especial interest for our present case that in the *Bṛihat Saṁhitā* by Varāhamihira (505—587), written about the middle of the sixth century, in which a summary of the Indian arts of divination is given, the auspicious or unlucky movements of crows are mentioned. [1]) A work of the type of *K.*, ac-

---

I even belong to those heretics who are still far from being convinced of the existence of such a thing as the *indogermanische urzeit*, — at least in that purely mechanical and subjective formula in which it is generally conceived. The work of Feist, however, is a laudable exception, perhaps the first sensible book written on this subject, and I read it from beginning to end with real pleasure. — In regard to the crow or raven, we find also other ideas connected with them than those of a soul-bird, in India as well as among other Indo-European peoples. In a legend connected with Rāma, an Asura disguised as a crow appears to peck at Sītā's breast (E. Thurston, *l. c.*, p. 276, and *Omens and Superstitions of Southern India*, p. 87, London, 1912). Among the southern Slavs, the crows are believed to be transformed witches (F. S. Krauss, *Slavische Volksforschungen*, pp. 57, 60, Leipzig, 1908); and in mediaeval legends, the devil occasionally assumes the shape of a raven. In Greek legend Apollo repeatedly appears in the disguise of a raven (O. Keller, *Die antike Tierwelt*, Vol. II, p. 108). These various examples demonstrate that the raven as a divine bird cannot be solely explained as the embodiment of an ancestral soul. It seems to me that H. Oldenberg (*Die Religion des Veda*, pp. 76, 510) is right in assuming that the animals sent by the gods were those of a weird, demoniacal nature, and were, for this reason, themselves deified, while at a later time they became mere stewards to divine mandators. "The bird crying in the quarter of the fathers" (the south), mentioned in the Ṛigveda, according to Oldenberg, should be understood as one being despatched by the fathers. The *document Pelliot* lends substantial force to this argument. It is there expressed in plain and unmistakable words that the raven is a divine bird of celestial origin and supernatural qualities, and the messenger who announces the will of a deity, the Venerable One of the Gods (*Lha btsun*); compare the Preface to the Table, translated below.

1) Ch. XLV is taken up by the auguries obtained from the wagtails (see H. Kern's translation in his *Verspreide geschriften*, Vol. I, p. 299, 's-Gravenhage, 1913; on crows, *ibid.*, pp. 130, 178). Regarding Varāhamihira's date of birth Mukerji in *J. A. S. B.*, 1912, pp. 275—8.

cordingly, must have been known at that time; but was it much earlier? I am under the impression that *K.* is hardly earlier than the sixth or seventh century, perhaps contemporaneous with the *Çākuna* of Vasantarāja, which, according to Hultzsch (p. 27), is posterior to Varāhamihira; the striking lack of thought and imagination, and the somewhat flat treatment of the subject, plainly stamp *K.* as a late production. The absence of any mythological detail is a decided drawback; the religious function of the crow is not even set forth, and we remain entirely in the dark as to the religious concept of the bird in the India of that period. Schiefner designated the little work a Buddhist retouch (*Überarbeitung*) of a Brahmanic text. It seems to me to be neither the one nor the other. It cannot be yoked to any definite religious system; it takes root in the domain of folk-lore, and closely affiliates with those manifold branches of divination which, independent of any particular form of religion, are widely diffused from the shores of the Mediterranean to almost the whole of continental Asia and the Malayan world. [1]) The tone and tenor of this text are not Buddhistic, nor

---

1) T. S. Raffles (*The History of Java*, Vol. II, p. 70, London, 1830) tells, in regard to the ancient Javanese, that when the crop was gathered and the accustomed devotions performed, the chief appointed the mode and time of the departure of the horde from one place to another. On these occasions, the horde, after offering their sacrifices and feasting in an open plain, left the remains of their repast to attract the bird *ílunggága* (supposed to have been a crow or raven); and the young men shook the *ánklung* (a rude instrument of music still in use), and set up a shout in imitation of its cry. If the bird did not eat of the meal offered to it, or if it afterwards remained hovering in the air, perched quietly on a tree, or in its flight took a course opposite to that which the horde wished to pursue, their departure was deferred, and their prayers and sacrifices renewed. But when the bird, having eaten of its meal, flew in the direction of their intended journey, the ceremony was concluded by slaying and burning a lamb, a kid, or the young of some other animal, as an offering of gratitude to the deity. Raffles adds that the Dayak of Borneo still hold particular kinds of birds in high veneration, and draw omens from their flight and the sounds which they utter. Before entering on a journey or engaging in war, head-hunting, or any matter of importance, they procure omens from a species of white-headed kite, and invite its approach by screaming songs, and scattering rice before it.

is there a particle of Buddhist color admixed with it. Nor is there in it much that could be styled specifically Indian, with the exception, of course, of the outward garb in which it is clothed; but most of the oracles could as well have been conceived in Greece or Rome.[1])

We may justly assume that *K.* was not the only work of its class, and that other Sanskrit books of an allied character may

---

If these birds take their flight in the direction they wish to go, it is regarded as a favorable omen; but if they take another direction, they consider it as unfavorable, and delay the business until the omens are more suitable to their wishes. See now Hose and McDougall, *The Pagan Tribes of Borneo*, Vol. I, pp. 168—170, Vol. II, p. 74 (London, 1912). Omens are taken either from the flight or the cries of certain birds, such as the night-owl, the crow, etc. (W. W. Skeat, *Malay Magic*, p. 535, London, 1900). Among the tribes of the Philippines, bird omens play an extensive rôle. My colleague F. C. Cole, who has studied to a great extent their religious notions, kindly imparts the following information on the subject: "With the Batak, a pigmy people living in northern Palawan, the small sun bird known as *sagwaysagway* is considered the messenger of Diwata [evidently Skr. *devatā*] Mendusa, the greatest of the nature spirits. Should this bird sing while they are on the trail, the Batak will return home, for evil is sure to follow if they continue their journey that day. Should the bird enter a dwelling and sing, the place is deserted. When a man desires to make a clearing in the jungle, he first addresses the sun bird, asking it to sing and give him the sign if it is a bad place to plant, but to be silent if it is a good plot for him to cultivate. Similar beliefs are entertained by the Tagbanua tribe which inhabits the greater part of Palawan." Further information will be found in the publication of F. C. Cole, *The Wild Tribes of Davao District, Mindanao*, pp. 63, 108, 153, 173 (*Field Museum Anthr. Ser.*, Vol. XII, 1913).

1) The Greeks distinguished five kinds of divination (*οἰωνιστική*) headed by auguration (*τὸ ὀρνεοσκοπικόν*); Telegonos was the first to write on this subject (H. Diels, *Beiträge zur Zuckungsliteratur des Okzidents und Orients* I, *Abhandl. preuss. Akad.*, 1908, p. 4). The typical Homeric method of foretelling the future was by the actions and cries of omen-birds. In Homer, the omen-bird is generally an eagle, and is always sent by Zeus, Apollo, or Athene. Its actions are symbolical, and need no complicated augury for their interpretation (Hastings, *Encyclopaedia of Religion*, Vol. IV, p. 787). In Aristophanes' Birds, Euelpides inquires what road is advised by a crow purchased at three obols. According to Virgil and Horace, a crow coming from the left-hand side is of ill omen. In Works and Days by Hesiod it is said, "Do not let a house incomplete, otherwise a garrulous crow will perch on it and caw." Even Epiktet believed in the correctness of the evil prophecies of a raven (O. Keller, *Die antike Tierwelt*, Vol. II, p. 97). Compare L. Hopf, *Tierorakel und Orakeltiere in alter und neuer Zeit* (Stuttgart, 1888); and W. R. Halliday, *Greek Divination, a Study of its Methods and Principles* (London, 1913).

then have existed in Tibet; [1]) for, with all the coincidences prevailing between *K.* and the *document Pelliot*, there are, on the other hand, far-reaching deviations extant in the latter which cannot be explained from *K.* First of all, however, the interdependence of the two texts should be insisted upon. The main subject of the two is identical; it is the method of obtaining omens from crows which is treated in both on the same principle. This principle is based on a combination of two elements, — orientation of the augur and time-reckoning according to the hours of the day; divination is determined by space and time. In regard to the division of space, the coincidence in the two documents is perfect; the nine [2]) points of the compass forming the framework in both are one and the same. Time calculation is likewise the same in principle, except that *K.* follows the Indian, the Table the Tibetan method, — a point discussed farther on. The ideas expressed by the oracles show far-reaching agreements in both, and move within the narrow boundaries of a restricted area; no great imagination is displayed in them, they are rather commonplace and philistine, even puerile, but this is all that could be expected from this class of prophecy intended for the *profanum volgus*. Another feature which *K.* and the document of Pelliot have in common is the method of divining from the nature of the cries of the crow, independent of space and

1) Writings of similar contents are still extant in modern Tibetan literature. Brian H. Hodgson (*The Phoenix*, Vol. I, 1870, p. 94), in a notice on the *Literature of Tibet*, mentions a book "Ditakh, by Chopallah [C'os dpal?] Lama, at Urasikh; to interpret the ominous croaking of crows, and other inauspicious birds."

2) The number nine plays a great rôle in systems of divination. In southern India, the belief prevails that ill luck will follow should an owl sit on the house-top, or perch on the bough of a tree near the house. One screech forebodes death; two screeches, success in any approaching undertaking; three, the addition by marriage of a girl to the family; four, a disturbance; five, that the hearer will travel. Six screeches foretell the coming of guests; seven, mental distress; eight, sudden death; and nine signify favorable results (E. Thurston, *Ethnographic Notes in Southern India*, p. 281, Madras, 1906; and *Omens and Superstitions of Southern India*, p. 66, London, 1912).

time. The last six verses (24—29) of the prefatory note correspond in meaning to the conclusion of *K.*: "When a crow sounds the tone *ka-ka,*" etc. It is a notable coincidence that in both texts five notes of the bird are enumerated in words imitative of its sounds, in *K.* conceived from an Indian point of view, in *document Pelliot* nationalized in a Tibetan garb. [1]) The character and quality of these tones, as well as the distinction between good and bad omens, necessarily lead to an effort toward reconciling the evil spirit which speaks through the organ of the bird. Offerings may counterbalance the mischievous effects of unlucky omens, — again a point on which the two texts are in harmony.

The differentiation of the two, in the first place, is due to a technical feature. The text of *K.* is a literary production and an analytic account. What is offered in the *document Pelliot* is an abstract of this divinatory wisdom worked up into convenient tabular form, manifestly with a view to handy and practical use. Any one who had encountered the necessary experience by observing a crow in a certain direction at a certain time of the day was enabled to

---

1) The number five is evidently suggested by the five elements, as shown by the five cries of the *pingalā,* a kind of owl, distinguished according to the five elements in the *Çākuna* of Vasantarāja (Hultzsch, *Prolegomena,* p. 70). The beliefs in the omens of the owl in modern India are well set forth by E. Thurston (*Omens and Superstitions of Southern India,* pp. 65—67). The enmity between crow and owl in Indian folk-lore deserves a word of comment in this connection. Jäschke (*Dictionary,* p. 374) refers to *Suvarṇaprabhāsasūtra* as describing the crow as an inveterate enemy of the owl. In the *Prajñādaṇḍa* ascribed to Nāgārjuna (ed. Chandra Das, p. 9, Darjeeling, 1896) occurs the saying: "Those formerly vanquished by an enemy do not wish any longer for friendship. Look how the crows set fire to the cave filled with owls and burn them to death." In the same book (p. 8), the crows are credited with the killing of snakes. Compare also *Subhāshitaratnanidhi* 185 (ed. Csoma). The animosity of the crow toward the owl seems to be based on the observation of a natural fact. C. B. Cory (*The Birds of Illinois and Wisconsin,* p. 548) has the following to say: "They seem to entertain an intense dislike to certain animals, especially an owl. Often the peaceful quiet of the woods is suddenly broken by the harsh excited 'cawing' of a flock of crows, who have discovered a bird of that species quietly enjoying his diurnal siesta, and the din rarely ceases until the hated bird has been driven from his concealment and forced to seek other quarters."

read from this Table at a moment's notice what consequence this event would entail on his person. The subject-matter, therefore, was arranged here somewhat differently; the offerings placed at the very end of *K.* make here the very opening, and justly so, because, in accordance with the practical purpose of the Table, it was essential for the layman, or rather the priest acting on his behalf, to ascertain the kind of reconciliatory offering in case of threatening ill luck.

The greater fulness of the Table constitutes one of the principal divergences from *K.* In the latter, only five divisions of day-time are presented, while the Table offers double this number. This is infallible proof for the fact that the divination process revealed by the *document Pelliot* has been Tibetanized; it is by no means a translation from Sanskrit, but an adaptation based on some Sanskrit work or works of the type of *K.*, and freely assimilated to Tibetan thought. The Indian division of the day is abandoned; and the designations of the Tibetan colloquial language, as they are still partially in use, [1]) have been introduced into the Table. It is self-evident that these ten periods are not equivalents of the three-hour Indian *yāma*, but correspond to a double hour as found in China. In logical sequence these determinations run from about one o'clock at night to about nine o'clock in the evening. The plain Tibetan names for the points of the compass are all retained, while the fancy Indian names appearing in *K.* are all dropped. An attempt at adaptation to Tibetan taste has been made in the oracles. The killing of a yak and heavy snowfalls, for instance, are affairs peculiar to Tibet. It is manifest also that the prognostics given in

1) See G. Sandberg, *Hand-book of Colloquial Tibetan*, p. 162 (Calcutta, 1894), and C. A. Bell, *Manual of Colloquial Tibetan*, p. 110 (Calcutta, 1905), where other terms also are included; also A. Desgodins, *Essai de grammaire thibétaine*, pp. 90—91 (Hongkong, 1899).

the Table, in a number of cases, are more definite and specific than those of *K.*, which are rather monotonous and wearisome by frequent repetition of the same statement. Such repetitions, it is true, occur also in the Table (II, 2 = IX, 8; II, 4 = IV, 7 = VII, 4; V, 6 = IX, 1; VIII, 6 = X, 3), and there is certainly no waste of inventive power or exertion of ingenuity in this whole system. Apparently it appealed to the people of Tibet, where kindred ideas may have been in vogue in times prior to the infusion of Indian culture, [1]) and it is to this popularity that we owe the composition

---

1) For the inhabitants of the Western and Eastern Women Kingdom, the latter a branch of the K'iang, perhaps akin to the Tibetans, were in possession of a system of bird divination, *niao pu* 鳥卜 (*Sui shu*, Ch. 83, and *T'ang shu*, Ch. 122; the two passages are translated by Rockhill, *The Land of the Lamas*, pp. 339, 341, the former also by Bushell, *The Early History of Tibet*, p. 97, *J. R. A. S.*, 1880), which was based on the examination of a pheasant's crop, — a process of divination certainly differing from what is described in our Tibetan texts. Nevertheless we may infer that the shamans of those peoples, especially as the *T'ang shu* states that to divine they go in the tenth month into the mountains scattering grain about and calling a flock of birds, paid a great deal of attention to birds. (Whether the inhabitants of the two Women Kingdoms spoke a Tibetan language seems doubtful. The *T'ang shu* has preserved to us three words of the language of the Eastern one: *pin-tsiu* 賓就 "sovereign" 王, *kao-pa-li* 高霸黎 "minister" 宰相, and *su-yi* 䩳𩍐 "shoe" 履. None of these is traceable to a Tibetan word known to us. The vocabulary is so widely different in the present Tibetan dialects that this may have been the case even in ancient times; at any rate, these three examples are not sufficient evidence for pronouncing a verdict. The word *su-yi* (not contained in Giles and Palladius) is explained by the *Shi ming* as quoted in K'ang-hi's Dictionary 胡中所名也 "a word employed among the *Hu*"). The *T'ang shu* (Ch. 216 下, p. 6 a) relates that the great sorcerers *po ch'é pu* 鉢掣逋 (exactly corresponding to Tib. *ąbà c'e-po*, "great sorcerer"), taking their place on the right-hand side of the Tibetan king, wore, during their prayer ceremonies, head-dresses in the shape of birds and girdles of tiger-skin (巫祝鳥冠虎帶), while beating drums. They certainly were shamans, as indicated by the very Chinese word *wu* and the style of their costume, and it is difficult to see what made Bushell (*The Early History of Tibet*, p. 101, note 81) think that the *po ch'é pu* would appear to have been a Buddhist. — Among the adherents of the Bon religion, transfiguration of saints into birds, and observation of and divination from birds' voices, are prominent (see *rGyal rabs bon-gyi ąbyuṅ gnas*, pp. 12, 13; regarding this work compare *T'oung Pao*, 1901, p. 24); there the verse occurs, "Omens are derived from birds, trees, the four elements, hills and rocks; from these the voices of the Bon doctrine have arisen."

of this divination table in the colloquial language. This point marks the fundamental importance of the *document Pelliot*, which thus becomes the earliest document of the Tibetan vernacular that we have at present. And it is no small surprise to notice that the style of this text is thoroughly identical with that of the living language of the present day. Any one familiar with it will testify to the fact that he can perfectly understand this Table through the medium of his knowledge of colloquial Tibetan. The safest criterion for the correctness of this diagnosis is furnished by M. BACOT himself, who had doubtless mastered Tibetan conversation during his journeyings in the country, and, I venture to assume, was considerably aided by this knowledge in grasping correctly the meaning of the oracles in the Table. But let us not wholly rely on such impressionistic opinions, when the text of *K.*, written in the Tibetan *wên li*, the style of the early Buddhist translators, offers such a tempting opportunity for comparing analogous sentences of the two texts. In *T.* (Table) all oracles are concluded with the plain verb *ston*; in *K. rtags-so* or the periphrastic future tense with *ạgyur-ro* are used, which do not occur in *T.* In *K.* we read *mes ạtsᶜig-par ạgyur-ro*, "a conflagration will break out;" the same is plainly expressed in *T.* by the words *mye ṅan žig oṅ-bar ston.* In *K. raṅ-gi ṅe-bo oṅ-bar ạgyur-ro*; the same in *T. gṅen žig oṅ-bar ston.* In *K. rluṅ cᶜen-po ạbyuṅ-bar ạgyur-ro*; the same in *T. rluṅ ldaṅ-bar ston*, etc. *T.* has the plain and popular words throughout, as *tᶜab-mo* for *ạkᶜrug-pa*, *bza bca* ("food and drink") for *bza daṅ skom-pa* in *K.*, and, as shown, in the names of the quarters and divisions of the day. Note that the termination *o* denoting the stop, and restricted to the written language (discussed farther on), is absent in *document Pelliot*; there is always *ston*, not *ston-no*, and at the end of the preface *ston yin.*

As to the time of the authorship of *document Pelliot*, there can be no doubt that in the same manner as *K.* it is a production of the ninth century. This is, first of all, proved by the date of *K.*, which at the time of its introduction and translation was a live source impressing the minds of the people, and hence gave the impetus to further developments of the subject in a manner tangible and palatable to the nation. Only at a time when the impression of these things was deep, and the practice of such beliefs was still fresh and vigorous, was the cast of these notions in the direct and plastic language of the people possible. Secondly, the antiquity of our document is evidenced by palaeographic and phonetic traits (discussed hereafter) occurring in other writings of equal age; it ranges in that period of language which is styled by the scholars of Tibet "old language" (*brda rñiṅ*). Thirdly, there is the circumstantial evidence, the discovery of the document in the cave of Tun-huang by M. Pelliot (see p. 2).

Let us note *en passant* that the Indian system of crow augury has been transmitted also to China. H. Doré in his excellent book "Recherches sur les superstitions en Chine" (pt. 1, Vol. II, p. 257, Shanghai, 1912), has revealed a Chinese text on bird divination which plainly betrays its connection with *K.* It is based in the same manner on the division of the day into five parts and on the local orientation of the cardinal points, eight of which are given by Doré. The presages are identical in tone with those of *K.* and *document Pelliot*; we meet predictions of wind and rain, disputes, threatening of a disaster, reception of a visit, death of a domestic animal, recovery of a lost object, malady, happy events, growth of fortune, gifts, arrival of a friend or a stranger, etc., without reference to any specific Chinese traits. [1])

1) In regard to beliefs in crow and raven in China, the reader may be referred to De Groot, *The Religious System of China*, Vol. V, pp. 638—640; J. F. Davis, *China*,

## The Preface to the Table.

As M. Bacot's rendering of the preface accompanying the Table is in need of a revision, I take the liberty to offer a new translation of it, [1]) discussing in the notes the chief points in which my opinion deviates from that of M. Bacot. A Lama, bsTan-pa du-ldan by name, has been consulted by this gentleman, and has jotted down for him a number of notes, explaining certain phrases in the colloquial language. These notes are reproduced on pp. 447—448 of the essay of M. Bacot, but apparently have not been utilized. Most of the Lama's comments are correct, a few are wrong, and some, though wrong, are yet interesting. Anything of interest in his explanations is embodied in the notes which follow. It may not be amiss to give here a transliteration of the text, in order to enable the reader to compare my translation with it immediately. In M. Bacot's edition, the text (in Tibetan characters) appears as prose; but it is very essential to recognize its metrical composition. The metre is rigorously adhered to in the twenty-nine verses, and is –́ ⏑ ⏑ –́ ⏑ –́ ⏑, a dactyl followed by two trochees (the signs – and ⏑ denote merely accentuated and unaccentuated, not long

---

Vol. II, p. 98 (London, 1857); J. Doolittle, *Social Life of the Chinese*, p. 571 (London, 1868). The subject is still in need of special investigation. Crows and ravens are certainly very far from being exclusively birds of ill omen or productive of evil, as De Groot is inclined to think; on the contrary, the raven was even the emblem of filial piety, and the appearance of one of red color was a lucky augury, foreboding the success of the Chou dynasty (Chavannes, *Les mémoires historiques de Se-ma Ts'ien*, Vol. I, p. 226). Other augur birds, as the mainah (Legge, *The Chinese Classics*, Vol. V, pt. II, p. 709; Watters, *Essays on the Chinese Language*, p. 444; and Forke, *Lun-hêng*, pt. II, p. 3) and the magpie, who knows the future (Forke, *l. c.*, pt. I, p. 358; pt. II, p. 126), must be equally taken into consideration.

1) In a bibliographical notice of M. Bacot's study (*Revue de l'histoire des religions*, 1913, p. 122) it is remarked, "Un curieux préambule mériterait d'être tiré au clair; mais il ne semble plus compris aujourd'hui."

and short syllables).[1] A. H. FRANCKE[2]) observes that in Ladākhi poetry the dactyl is rather frequent, arising from a dissyllabic compound with a suffix. This certainly holds good of all Tibetan dialects and also of the written language. In this composition, all the dactyls are formed by the particle *ni* coupled with a trochaic element. It is curious that all verses are constructed in the same manner, having this *ni* in the third syllable (compare note to V. 19). At the same time, there is obviously a cesura after *ni*.[3])

## Text of the Preface.

(The accents denote the metre.)

1 *pʻó-rog ni myí-i mgón*
2 *dráṅ-sroṅ ni lhá-i bká*
3 *byáṅ ąbrog ni ąbróṅ ša-i rkyén*
4 *yúl-gi ni dbús mtʻil dú*
5 *lhá btsun ni bdá* (+ *a*)[4]) *skad skyél*
6 *pʻyógs brgyad ni ltéṅ daṅ dgú*
7 *,áṅ toṅ ni tʻábs gsum gsúṅs*
8 *gtór-ma ni byá-la gtór*

---

1) On Tibetan metrics compare H. BECKH, *Beiträge zur tibetischen Grammatik, Lexikographie und Metrik* (*Anhang zu den Abhandl. der preussischen Akademie*, 1908, pp. 53—63). The author justly emphasizes that in the study of Tibetan works the metre is to be investigated in the first line, and that it should be kept in mind in all text-critical and grammatical questions; but he overlooks the fact that this principle had been fully brought into effect by the present writer in *Ein Sühngedicht der Bonpo* (*Denkschriften Wiener Akademie*, 1900), where textual criticism is fundamentally based on metrical considerations and statistical tables of the various metres.

2) *Sketch of Ladakhi Grammar*, p. 7 (Calcutta, 1901).

3) My reading of the text is based only on the edition of M. BACOT, the general accuracy of which there is no reason to doubt. Not having had the privilege of checking it with the original, I do not hold myself responsible for eventual errors which may have crept in there. In V. 20, *gsaṅ*, printed in M. BACOT's text, is apparently a misprint for *gsan*; *lhiṅ* (V. 24), for *lteṅ* (as in V. 6).

4) This graphic peculiarity is explained below, under the heading "Palaeographic Traits."

9 *ts$^c$ó-ts$^c$o ni yóṅs-su gyís*

10 *lhá-i ni p$^c$yág-du ạbúl*

11 *grágs dgu-r ni ltás myi bltá* (+ *a*) [1])

12 *bzáṅ ṅan ni ltás-su gsúṅ*

13 *dráṅ-sroṅ ni lhá ạdsin lá*

14 *lhá ston ni gñén-bai byá* (+ *a*) [1])

15 *mú sman ni gñén-gis gsúṅs*

16 *dráṅ žiṅ ni brtán-por stón*

17 *p$^c$ó-rog ni dgúṅ-gi byá*

18 *ạdáb drug ni gšóg drug pá* (+ *a*) [1])

19 *lhá yul ni mt$^c$ó-du p$^c$yín*

20 *dmyíg rno ni sñán gsan bás*

21 *lhá-i ni mán-ṅag stón*

22 *myí rtog ni gcíg-ma mc$^c$ís*

23 *yíd c$^c$es ni séms rton cíg*

24 *p$^c$yóys brgyad ni ltéṅ daṅ dgú*

25 *lhóṅ lhoṅ ni bzáṅ-por stón*

26 *t$^c$ág t$^c$ag ni ạbríṅ-du stón*

27 *krág krag ni ríṅs-par stón*

28 *króg krog ni gróg yoṅs smrá*

29 *,iú ,iu ni bár ston yín.*

## Translation.

1 The Raven is the protector of men,

2 And the officiating priest (carries out) the order of the gods.

4 (Sending him, the Raven) into the middle of the country,

3 Where he has occasion for feeding on yak-flesh in the outlying pasture-lands,

5 The Venerable of the Gods conveys (his will) by means of the sound-language (of the Raven).

---

1) This graphic peculiarity is explained below under the heading "Palaeographic Traits."

6 When in the eight quarters, making nine with the addition of the zenith,

7 He (the Raven) sounds his notes, the three means (to be observed) are explained as follows:

8 The offering must be presented to the bird (the Raven),

9 And it should be a complete feeding in each instance.

10 (In this manner, the offering) is given into the hands of the god (or gods).

11 As to the omens, they are not drawn from the mere cries (of the Raven),

12 But in the announcement of the omens a distinction is made between good and evil cries.

13 The officiating priest is in possession of the knowledge of the gods,

14 He teaches (the orders of) the gods, and it is the bird who is his helpmate (in this task).

15 The remedies for warding off the demons are announced by the helpmate.

16 Truthful in his speech, he proves trustworthy,

17 For the Raven is a bird of Heaven;

18 He is possessed of six wings and six pinions.

19 Thanks to his visits above in the land of the gods,

20 His sense of sight is keen, and his hearing is sharp.

21 (Hence he is able) to teach (mankind) the directions of the gods.

22 There is for man but one method of examining (the sounds of the Raven),

23 And may you hence have faith and confidence (in his auguries)!

24 In the eight quarters, making nine with the addition of the zenith, (the following sounds of the Raven occur:)

25 The sound *lhoṅ lhoṅ* foretells a lucky omen.

26 The sound *tʿag tʿag* forebodes an omen of middle quality.

27 The sound *krag krag* foretells the coming of a person from a distance.

28 The sound *krog krog* announces the arrival of a friend.

29 The sound *,iu ,iu* is an augury of any future event (as indicated in the Table).

---

## NOTES.

V. 1. The raven *pʿo-rog* is still called *cʿos skyoṅ* (Skr. *dharmapāla*), "protector of religion" (G. Sandberg, *Hand-book of Colloquial Tibetan*, p. 170). The word *mgon* is employed in the sense of Sanskrit *nātha*. Our text gives the word only in the form *pʿo-rog*, while in *K.* the form *bya-rog* is used exclusively. The latter, as shown by *Mahāvyutpatti*, seems to be the recognized form of the written language, while *pʿo-rog* seems to be more popular; the latter occurs, for example, in the Tibetan prose version of the *Avadānakalpalatā*, which has been written for children. The distinction of *bya-rog* as "crow," and *pʿo-rog* as "raven," is based on the Sanskrit-Tibetan dictionary *Amarakosha* (T. Zachariae, *Die indischen Wörterbücher*, p. 18), where Tib. *bya-rog* is the equivalent of Skr. *vāyasa* ("crow"), and Tib. *pʿo-rog* that of Skr. *droṇa* ("raven"), the two words being treated in different stanzas (ed. of Vidyābhūṣaṇa, *Bibl. ind.*, p. 184, Calcutta, 1911).

The word *bya-rog* appears twice in the *Mahāvyutpatti*, section on birds (Tanjur, Sūtra, Vol. 123, fols. 265b, 266a, Palace edition), — first, as translation of Skr. *dhvāṅksha*, "crow" (in *Amarakosha* rendered by *sgra ldan*), where the synonyms *spyi-brtol-can* (the Palace edition writes *sbyi-rtol-can*), "the impudent one," and *kʿva*, are added; second, as rendering of Skr. *droṇakāka*, "raven," while the Skr. *kāka* and *vāyasa* are rendered by Tib. *wa* (not noted with this meaning in our dictionaries), evidently an imitative sound, in the same manner as Tib. *kʿva*, *kʿva-ta*, and *kʿa-ta*, "raven," and *ko-wag*, a word expressive of the voice of the raven. In *Se tʿi tsʿing wên kien* 四體清文鑑 (Ch. 30, p. 25) the following distinctions are made: *kʿa-ta* corresponds to *wu-ya* 烏鴉, Manchu *gaha*, Mongol *käryä*; Tib. *bya-rog*, to *tsʿe-ya* 慈鴉, Manchu *holon gaha*, Mongol *khong käryä*; Tib. *pʿo-rog*, to *hua po ya* 花脖鴉 ("raven with colored neck"), Manchu *ayan gaha*, Mongol *torok käryä*. In the Appendix to this dictionary (Ch. 4, p. 12) we find Tib. *bya-rog* = *kuan* 鸛 (according to Giles a species of stork), Manchu *śungkeri gôwara* (according to Sacharov a kind of large horned owl); and Tib. *ka-ka* = *hu kʿua ying* 呼咵鷹, Manchu *hurkun gôwara*. In these two cases the Tibetan names seem to be artificial productions made *ad hoc* in order to translate the Manchu words. The *Polyglot List of Birds in Turki, Manchu and Chinese*, published by E. D. Ross (*Mem. A. S. B.*, Vol. II, No. 9, 1909), though in general a useful work, is incomplete in that the Appendix of the Polyglot Dictionary, containing about two hundred more names of birds, has not been utilized at all. For future work of this kind the following suggestions may be offered in regard to the methods of obtaining identifications of bird-names. In my opinion, it is an incorrect procedure, in most cases, to try to identify any Oriental bird-name with a *species* of our own ornithological nomenclature, because our scientific research has made out infinitely more species of birds than there are words for the species in any language; all we can hope for, at the best, is to establish the *genus*, and in many cases we have to be content to ascertain the family. Take, for example, the case of crow or raven, a popular name embracing a large family of birds, *Corvidae*. In 1877 A. DAVID and M. E. OUSTALET (*Les oiseaux de la Chine*, p. 366) stated that nearly two hundred species of it were known on the globe, and twenty-seven from China. At present we certainly know many more in addition. (A. LAUBMANN, *Wissenschaftliche Ergebnisse der Reise von G. Merzbacher*, *Abhandlungen der bayerischen Akademie*, 1913, pp. 37—42, enumerates ten genera of the family *Corvidae* from the region of the T'ien Shan.) Who can name those twenty-seven species in Chinese? Nobody. Our species are made from points of view which are entirely foreign to the minds of Oriental peoples. They see different "kinds," where our ornithologist may establish one species; and they may have one word, where we are forced to admit different species, and even *genera*; and they may even take the male and female of the same species for two distinct birds. It is further necessary to disillusion our minds regarding the production of the K'ien-lung lexicographers, which must be handled with great caution and pitiless criticism: it teems with artificial makeshifts in Manchu, Tibetan, and Mongol, which are not genuine constituents of these languages, and is vitiated by numerous blunders in spelling, which are to be corrected. The compilers were philologists, not zoölogists; and their combinations of bird-names in the various languages offer no guaranty that these refer to really identical *genera*, not to speak of *species*, the greater probability in each case being that the species are entirely different (thus, for instance, as may be determined, in the majority of Tibetan and Chinese bird-names). — Tib. *bya rog* means "the black bird," and *p'o-rog* "the male black one." There is a dialectic form *,o-rog*, *,o-lag* (WALSH, *Vocabulary of the Tromowa Dialect of Tibetan*, pp. 11, 28, Calcutta, 1905), with the prefixed *,a* (here *,o* in consequence of vowel-attraction) forming nouns (SCHIEFNER, *Mélanges asiatiques*, Vol. I, p. 362; and MAINWARING, *Grammar of the Róng* [*Lepcha*] *Language*, p. 111). In meaning and grammatical formation this *,o-rog* corresponds to Lolo *a-nye*, "the black one," *i. e.* the raven (*T'oung Pao*, 1912, p. 13). The common raven, somewhat larger than the European species, is ubiquitous in

Tibet. Some remarks on it are made by P. LANDON (*Lhasa*, Vol. I, p. 404, London, 1905). According to H. v. SCHLAGINTWEIT (*J. R. A. S.*, 1863, p. 15), it occurs even in the ice-regions of the greatest elevation of the Himālaya: "some of the species of *corvus tibetanus* accompanied us during our ascent of the Ibi Gamin peak up to our highest encampment at 19,326 feet." Of especial interest with reference to the present case is the following observation of THOMAS MANNING, who travelled in Tibet 1811—12 (C. R. MARKHAM, *Narratives of the Mission of George Bogle to Tibet*, etc., p. 249, London, 1876): "Many of the ravens about this lake, and many in Lhasa, emit a peculiar and extraordinary sound, which I call metallic. It is as if their throat was a metal tube, with a stiff metal elastic musical spring fixed in it, which, pulled aside and let go, should give a vibrating note, sounding like the pronunciation of the word *poing*, or *scroong*, with the lips protruded, and with a certain musical accent. The other is similar to that of the ravens in Europe, yet still has something of the metallic sound in it. Whether there be two species of ravens here, or whether it be that the male and female of the same species have each their peculiar note, I cannot say."

V. 2. Who is the *drań-sroń* (corresponding to Skr. *ṛishi*)? The Lama bsTan-pa du-ldan, whose explanatory notes in Tibetan have been published by M. BACOT, on p. 447 comments that the raven *p'o-rog* is "the raven staying near the head of Vishṇu," and that Vishṇu should be understood by the term *ṛishi*. It is certainly the mythical bird Garuḍa, being the vehicle (*vāhana*) of Vishṇu, which crossed the Lama's mind, and it will be demonstrated farther on (V. 18) that an assimilation between Raven and Garuḍa has indeed taken place in Tibet (in the *Çākuna* of Vasantarāja the Garuḍa commands the *kāka* as an omen-bird: HULTZSCH, *Prolegomena*, p. 41). The beginnings of such an adjustment are visible even in our text when, in V. 17—18, it is said that the Raven is a bird of Heaven, and possessed of six wings and six pinions; he is, in a word, looked upon as a solar bird. Nevertheless, he is not identical with the Garuḍa, and I do not believe that the Lama's explanation is correct. Above all, *drań-sroń* cannot be identified with Vishṇu or any other god; for he is the person who executes the orders of the gods (V. 2; in this sense, at least, it seems to me, the passage should be understood), who has the knowledge of the gods (*lha ądsin*, V. 13), and who teaches the gods (*lha ston*, V. 14). The Raven is his helpmate (*gñen-pa*, V. 14), and he announces the will and the wishes of the gods transmitted by the divine bird. The *drań-sroń*, accordingly, is a person with a priestly function; and I should almost feel tempted to propose for the word, in this case, the translation "seer" or "augur." It is the *çākunika* of the Sanskrit texts who is designated also *guru* and *ācārya* (HULTZSCH, *Prolegomena*, p. 6). Moreover, we know that the word *drań-sroń* has obtained among the Lamas a meaning like "officinting priest, sacrificant,"

JÄSCHKE (*Dictionary*, p. 261) states *sub voce*, "At present the Lama that offers *sbyin-sreg* [a burnt-offering, Skr. *homa*] is stated to bear that name, and while he is attending to the sacred rites, he is not allowed to eat anything but *dkar-zas* [white food, like milk, curd, cheese, or butter]." Inevitably we must assume that our Table was not directly used by the laity, but that it was placed in charge of a priest who had due control over supernatural events. The layman who had encountered the vision of a raven applied to him for the proper oracle to be ascertained from the chart, and particularly, if necessary, for the making of the required offering, which was a ritual act along established rules. The Lama who fulfilled this function was called the *drań-sroń*. The origin of this word is explained in the work *sGra sbyor* (quoted above, p. 19; Tanjur, Sūtra, Vol. 124, fol. 6b) by the sentence *kāya-vāk-manobhir-ṛiju-çete iti ṛishi*, rendered into Tibetan thus: *lus dań ńag dań yid droń-por gnas-šiń sroń-bas-na drań-sroń c'en-po žes btags*, "he who in regard to his body (actions), speech, and heart, remains straight and keeps them straight, is designated a great Ṛishi." Hence it follows that in the minds of the Tibetans the compound *drań-sroń* is formed of the words *drań-po* (Skr. *ṛiju*, "straight," in the literal and moral sense) and the verb *sroń-ba*, "to straighten," and that the Tibetan interpretation is "one who is straight, upright in his conduct." Another definition given in the same work is "one who is possessed of knowledge" (*šes-pa-dań-ldan-pa*). The notion of "hermit" given in our Tibetan dictionaries is apparently not implied in the Tibetan definitions. It will thus be noticed that the literal interpretation of the word, "one who straightens out affairs in a straight manner," could result in the development of the notion "one who straightens out affairs relating to sacrifice, augury or divination."

V. 3. Tib. *byań ąbrog* is identified by M. BACOT with the well-known term *byań t'ań*, "the northern table-lands." The two expressions are evidently synonymous (compare VASILYEV, *Geography of Tibet*, in Russian, p. 11, St. Pet., 1895). *Byań ąbrog* appears as one of the thirteen districts assigned by the Mongol emperors to the hierarchs of Sa-skya (*dPag bsam ljon bzań*, p. 159, l. 1); but I do not believe that a definite locality in the geographical sense is here intended, any more than I believe that the word *dbus* ("centre") in the following verse need refer particularly to the Tibetan province of that name. The term *byań t'ań* is also a general designation for uncultivated pastoral high lands (the proper meaning of *t'ań* is not "plain, steppe," as given in our dictionaries, but "plateau"), in opposition to *roń t'ań*, the low lands of the valleys. The former is the habitat of pastoral tribes; the latter, the seat of the agriculturists. The first element in *byań t'ań*, in all likelihood, was not originally the word *byań*, "north," but the word *ljań*, "green" (*byań* and *ljań* are both sounded *jań*; *ljań t'ań*, "green plateau," is the name of a province in mNa-ris ṇK'or-gsum, according to H. v. SCHLAGINTWEIT, *Glossary of Tibetan Geographical Terms*, *J. R. A. S.*, Vol. XX, 1863, p. 13); for in Ladākh, for instance, the people apply the word *byaṅ t'aṅ* to the district of Ru-tog, situated on their eastern border, in the sense that it is more bleak and unreclaimed than their own sheltered and less elevated valleys (compare H. STRACHEY, *J. A. S. B.*, Vol. XVII, 1848, p. 331). The same evidently holds good for our text, for, in understanding *byaṅ ạbrog* literally, it would be unintelligible why the Raven despatched into the centre of the country should be supposed to gain his livelihood in the pastures of the north. The "centre," it should be understood, may be any settlement in Tibet with a sedentary farming population; and the term *byaṅ ạbrog* may refer to any nomadic district in its proximity where the Raven stands a better chance for his food than among the husbandmen. The word "centre" is probably chosen in view of the nine quarters which come into question for the Raven's flight; he has to start from a centre to make for the various directions. In regard to man, the cultivated land is conceived of as being centrally located, and surrounded on its outskirts by the wild mountains with their grassy plateaus suitable for cattle-raising. The tribal and social division of the Tibetan people into these two distinct groups of agriculturists and cattle-breeders meets its outward expression in the juxtaposition of the word-groups denoting „valley" and „mountain" („pasture," „plateau"), the one pertaining to cultivation, the other to everything uncultivated or of wild nature. The "valley pig" (*luṅ p'ag*) is the domestic pig, a sedentary animal found only among the farmers, but never among the nomads; while the "mountain pig" (*ri p'ag*) is the wild boar: hence *ri* and abbreviated into the prefix *r-*, with predilection, enters into the names of wild animals (*W. Z. K. M.*, Vol. XIII, 1900, p. 206).

In regard to the yak-flesh we may remember the passage of the *T'ang shu* (BUSHELL, *The Early History of Tibet*, p. 7): "When they entertain envoys from foreign countries, they always bring out a yak for the guest himself to shoot, the flesh of which is afterwards served at the banquet." In the legends of the Buryat, the crow is invited by people to take part in a meal furnished by a slaughtered ox (CHANGALOV and ZATOPL'AYEV, Бурятскія сказки и повѣрья, pp. 17, 21, Irkutsk, 1889).

V. 5. Tib. *lha btsun*, correctly translated by M. BACOT "le dieu vénérable," would correspond to Skr. *devabhadanta*. It is notable that the coming of *lha btsun* is the very first prediction appearing in the Table when the raven's voice sounds in the east during the first watch. His name appears again in Table VII, 6, where it is said that "the helper, or the assistance of the Venerable One (*btsun-pai-gñen*), will come." (I do not believe with M. BACOT that these words mean „un parent de distinction." In fact, M. BACOT sides with me in this opinion, for in Table V, 3, he very aptly and correctly renders the term *gñen lha* by „dieu protecteur"). The helper is referred to in V. 15 (*gñen*), and the expression *gñen-bai bya* ("the helping bird") in V. 14 leaves no doubt that the raven is meant. It seems futile for the present to speculate on the nature of this deity called *lha btsun*. All we may infer from this text is, that he seems to be a supreme god presiding over the *lha*, that he resides in the region of the gods (*lha yul*, V. 19), and that he reveals his will to mankind through the Raven, his messenger, whom he sends down on earth. On the whole, I am inclined to regard this deity as a native Tibetan concept, not as an adaptation to an Indian notion; possibly he is identical with the Spirit of Heaven 天神 invoked by the Tibetan shamans, according to *Kiu Tᶜang shu* (Ch. 196 上, p. 1b). — As regards the name *lha btsun*, an analogous expression is met in Taoism in the name of the deity Tᶜien tsun 天尊 (or Yüan shi Tᶜien tsun, the first of the three divinities forming the trinity of the Three Pure Ones 三清); Tib. *lha* and Chin. *tᶜien* correspond in meaning, both serving for the translation of Skr. *deva*; and Tib. *btsun* and Chin. *tsun*, as already recognized by ABEL-RÉMUSAT and SCHIEFNER (*Mélanges asiatiques*, Vol. I, p. 340), are identical words.

M. BACOT translates, "Le dieu vénérable accompagne la parole qu'il prend avec lui," by taking *bda* for the verb *bda-ba*. Even granted that the latter could have this meaning, the construction of the sentence remains ungrammatical, and the rendering gives no sense. In these ancient texts we must be mindful of the fact that spellings at variance with modern usage occur, or, in other words, that different phonetic conditions are fixed in writing. There is no difficulty in seeing that *bda* here stands for the common mode of writing *brda*; and *brda skad* is a very frequent compound, which, as correctly interpreted by JÄSCHKE, means (1) language expressed by signs or gestures, (2) language expressed by words. Here it refers to the prophetic sounds or language of the Raven by means of which the Venerable One of the Gods conveys (*skyel*) his will and wishes.

V. 6. In the commentary of the Lama (p. 447), where the verses of the text, which are explained, are repeated in larger type, this verse terminates with the word *bcu*, so that the Lama brings out ten quarters, adding the nadir ("the region of the *klu*, the land below") as the tenth; but this is evidently a slip which occurred in the copy taken by or for the Lama.

V. 7. The expression *‚añ toñ* presents some difficulties, as it is evidently an archaic and antiquated term not recorded in our dictionaries. The Lama maintains silence about it. M. BACOT has tentatively proposed to take it in the sense of *‚añ dañ-po*, and renders the sentence, "Le meilleur est d'énoncer les trois moyens." But this is an entirely un-Tibetan way of speaking, and M. BACOT's conception of the sentence contradicts the iron rules of Tibetan word-position. Such a translation would only be permissible if the reading were *t'abs gsum gsuṅs ,aṅ daṅ-po (red)*. Aside from this, the identification of *,aṅ toṅ* with *,aṅ daṅ* is hardly acceptable; it is not supported by any native dictionary, nor can it be upheld by any phonetic law. Further, the Sanskrit-Tibetan hybrid, in the written language usually *,aṅ-gi daṅ-po* (more rarely *,aṅ daṅ*), has only the meaning of the ordinal numeral "the first" (in the enumeration of a series), while in the sense of "first quality, best," it is a very vulgar expression of the colloquial language, about the equivalent of Pidgin-English "number one." A few considerations may place us on the right track as to the meaning of the phrase. The preceding verse, "in the eight quarters etc.," demands a verb; in looking up the parallel passages of *K.*, we notice that each of the determinations of the quarters is followed there by the words *skad sgrogs na*, "if (the crow) sounds its voice," and this is what is apparently required and intended in this passage. In this case we recognize in *toṅ* the verb *gtoṅ* (compare *sod* for *gsod* in Table II, 8; VI, 2, and the phonetic remarks below), which, as shown by JÄSCHKE (*Dictionary*, pp 19a, 209a), is indeed used in this sense in Ladākhi: *skad taṅ-ce*, "to utter sounds;" *ku-co, bó-ra taṅ-ce*, "to raise, to set up a cry." But the phrase in question occurs also in writing, like many others given by JÄSCHKE as dialectic expressions; a number of those could be compiled from the prose version of *Avadānakalpalatā*. The word *,aṅ* (probably derived from the Sanskrit particle *aṅga*, *pw.* "anrufend oder auffordernd") means "cry, clamor." SARAT CHANDRA DAS (*Dictionary*, p. 1347) cites an example of this kind, without translating it, in the sentence *mi-yis bos kyaṅ ,aṅ mi k'ug*, which evidently means, "Although the man called, his cries did not draw any attention." GOLSTUNSKI, in his Монголско-русскій словарь (Vol. I, p. 7b), assigns to Mongol *aṅ*, which has several other meanings, also the significance "shouting of fighters, cries of camels and donkeys." It is the same thing when JÄSCHKE quotes *,aṅ* as an interjection with the meaning "well, then! now, then! eh bien!" It is an exclamation. Another use of *,aṅ* not noticed heretofore seems to be traceable to the same origin. *,Aṅ* appears as a particle joined to the imperative with or without *cig*, as well as to the prohibitive. In *Bya c'os* (see note to V. 28), p. 39, we meet five times with *śog ,aṅ*. In *sLob gñer byed ts'ul-gyi bslab bya le ts'an gñis*, a small work published by the monastery Kumbum (*sKu ąbum*), we have *sgrims śig ,aṅ* (fol. 6), *gnas-par gyis śig ,aṅ* (fol. 7), *ma byed ,aṅ* (fol. 10), *ma rgyugs ,aṅ* (fol. 14), and many other examples. The meaning seems to correspond to French *donc* (German *doch*) in connection with an imperative, and this application seems to be derived from the original significance "cry, exclamation." In the case above, *,aṅ* is used as a noun synonymous with the word *skad* of *K.*, and refers to the cries of the raven which he emits (*gtoṅ*) in his flight toward the various quarters. The phrase *,aṅ toṅ* linked to the preceding verse is the psychological subject governed by *t'abs gsum gsuṅs*: the augury derived from the sounds of the raven voiced in the eight quarters is explained as consisting of three means or modes of procedure. The explanation is inspired by the Venerable of the Gods. The three means are the offering (*gtor-ma*, Skr. *bali*), the discrimination between good and evil cries (and accordingly auguries), and the oracle proclaimed by the priest, with his superior knowledge of the supernatural.

V. 8. Tib. *gtor-ma gtor-ba* (as *ltas lta-ba* in V. 11) is a hendiadys favorite in Tibetan and other Indo-Chinese languages. A. CONRADY (*Eine indochinesische Causativ-Denominativ-Bildung*, p. 81, Leipzig, 1896) has given a number of good examples of this kind; others occur in *Ein Sühngedicht der Bonpo*, *l. c.*, p. 27. Compare the synonyms of the crow given in *Amarakosha* (*l. c.*), — *balipushṭa* and *balibhuj*, — and the Tibetan synonyms *gtor-mas rgyas* and *gtor za* in the "Dictionary of the French Missionaries," p. 86. Several others enumerated in the latter may be explained from *Amarakosha*: as *ąc'i-med* = *arishṭa*; *gžan gso* = *parabhṛid*; *lan cig skyes* = *sakṛitpraja*, which accordingly does not mean "né une seule fois," but "one bearing young but once a year;" *bdag sgrog* (in the translation of *Amarakosha*, *sgrogs-pai bdag-ñid-can*) = *ātmaghosha*.

V. 9. M. BACOT translates, "Plus il y en a d'espèces, mieux cela vaut." He seems to have thought of *ts'o* ("number, host"), but, as already remarked by JÄSCHKE, this word hardly ever stands alone; in fact, it is only used as a suffix denoting a plural. As shown by the context, *ts'o* is written for *ąts'o* ("to feed, nourish"), and the duplication indicates the repeated action. Also the Lama, as shown by the wording of his comment, takes *ts'o* as a verb by saying that all birds *ts'o-nas* eat the offering; but, as he merely repeats *ts'o* in the same spelling as in the text, it is not clear in which sense he understands the verb. *Gyis* certainly is the imperative of *bgyid-pa*. V. 8 and 10 have been correctly rendered by M. BACOT.

V. 10. The Lama understands this verse, "The raven is a bird soaring in the sky" (*nam ldiṅ-gi bya*), and possibly thinks again of the Garuḍa. It seems to me that the Raven as a bird of Heaven is understood to be the messenger sent down from heaven, as previously set forth, and it implies also that he is of celestial origin, as specified in V. 19.

V. 11. Tib. *grags* is not used here in the sense of „glory," but with the literal meaning "cry, outcry, clamor;" it is derived from the verb *s-grog-pa*, ("to call, to shout"), which is identical with Chinese *kiao* 叫 ("to call out; the cries of certain animals and birds"), in the same manner as Tib. *s-grog-pa* ("to bind") = Chin. *kiao* 絞 ("to bind"), and Tib. *ą-grogs-pa* (from *grogs*, "friend, to be associated") = Chin. *kiao* 交, "to be united, friendship, intercourse" (compare A. Conrady, *Eine indochinesische Causativ-Denominativ-Bildung*, pp. VII, VIII, Leipzig, 1896). *Hua i yi yü* (Hirth's copy in the Royal Library of Berlin, Ch. 11, p. 67b) correctly renders Tibetan *grag* by *ming* 鳴. — Tib. *dgur* is not the word "crooked," as M. Bacot thinks, but is to be analyzed into *dgu-r*, terminative of *dgu* ("nine, many"), and particle expressing the plural (Foucaux, *Grammaire de la langue tibétaine*, p. 27; A. Schiefner, *Ueber Pluralbezeichnungen im Tibetischen*, § 23, in *Mém. Acad. de St.-Pétersbourg*, Vol. XXV, No. 1, 1877). The question may be raised whether *grags-dgu* denotes the various kinds of cries of the raven, of an indefinite number, or whether exactly nine sounds are understood. It would be rather tempting to assume the latter possibility, and to set the nine sounds in relation with the nine quarters; but at the end of the Preface only five sounds of the raven are enumerated in accordance with *K.* Again, the fact that this section of the Preface is preceded by the verse, "In the eight quarters, making nine with the zenith," leads one to think that, besides the series of five, a series of nine sounds, corresponding to the nine quarters, may have simultaneously existed, and that the matter is confused in this text. A positive decision on this point, however, cannot be reached, and I prefer to regard *dgu* as a mere designation of the plural.

V. 12. As plainly stated in the first horizontal column of the Table, an offering is necessary whenever the voice of the Raven sounds ill luck. M. Bacot translates this verse, "Le bon et le mauvais, après qu'on l'a vu, qui en parle?" He accordingly accepts *su* as interrogative pronoun, while it is evidently the particle of the terminative belonging to *ltas.* Such slips are certainly excusable, and have been committed by other translators. Thus, for example, E. Schlagintweit (*Die Lebensbeschreibung von Padma Sambhava* II, *Abhandl. der bayerischen Akad.*, 1903, p. 547) took the final *s-o*, denoting the stop, as the noun *so* ("tooth"), and translated the sentence *paṇḍita-rnams kun-gyis ma tʻub grags-so mtsʻams ạbyed-pas*, "All pandits praised him as the powerful one of the Abhidharma; if a tooth is hollow, its removal is desirable." There is nothing to this effect in the Tibetan words, which simply mean, "He is known under the name 'the One Unexcelled by all Pandits;' he began solitary meditation," etc. In the same author's *Die tibetischen Handschriften der k. Hof- und Staatsbibliothek zu München* (*Sitzungsberichte der bayerischen Akad.*, 1875, p. 73) occurs, in the title of a book, "the tooth of the fulfilment of the great Lama Rig-ạdsin;" the Tibetan *bskaṅ-so*, of course, is a mere graphic variant of *bskaṅs-so*, and means "the fulfilment of vows."

V. 14. M. Bacot takes *gñen-bai bya* in the sense of "devoir des parents." It may be granted that these words could have such a meaning, though as a rule *bya-ba* retains its suffix, when it has the rôle of the word assigned to it by M. BACOT. But the point is that such a viewing of the matter has no sense in this context. I should think that *bya* is simply "bird," as it occurred in V. 8; while the suffix *bai* or *pai* sufficiently indicates the verbal character of *gñen*, "to help, assist" (in its sense somewhat synonymous with *mgon*, V. 1). The whole term is to be construed like a Sanskrit Bahuvrīhi: the *Draṅ-sroṅ* is one having the bird as a helper. The fact that the helper refers to the Raven is manifest also from the following verse.

V. 15. M. BACOT translates, "remède de douleur, parole des parents." The meaning of *gñen* (V. 5) has been explained. The construction of the sentence is simple: in regard to the remedies, they are announced or explained by the helper (the Raven). The only difficulty is presented by the word *mu* preceding *sman*. Also M. BACOT has clearly seen that the word *mu* ("border, limit," etc.) cannot here come into question. In my opinion, we have to apply the rule laid down under V. 5, that a prefix has been dropped in *mu*; and I should like to propose to read *dmu* or *rmu* "evil demon," which befits the case very well; *dmu* is a demon causing blindness, dropsy, and other infirmities. In the Table (X, 1) the coming of demons is indicated as an oracle, and the augur is certainly obliged also to announce the means of escaping the evil effects or consequences of an oracle. In a wider sense, *mu sman*, accordingly, signifies the remedies releasing the person concerned from any threatening calamity in consequence of a prediction.

V. 16. This verse is explained by our Lama commentator (p. 442), "He who does not tell lies is reckoned as good by all men," which fairly reproduces the general sense, while the translation of M. BACOT is untenable. He takes *draṅ žiṅ* in the sense of "en conduisant," and accordingly derives it from the verb *ạdren-pa*; but "en conduisant" could be expressed only by *ạdren žiṅ*. The descriptive particle *ciṅ* is hardly ever joined to a future tense (no example from literature is known to me), usually to a present tense; in the majority of cases to an adjective, rarely to a past tense (compare the examples in the grammars of FOUCAUX, p. 19, and JÄSCHKE, p. 56). The chances, as a rule, are that the word preceding *ciṅ* is an adjective with verbal force. As such it is used here, *draṅ* standing for *draṅ-po* (any suffixes may be dropped in verse), "honest, upright, truthful," and this attribute refers to the truthful sound-language of the raven. The phrase *brtan-por ston* cannot mean „on montre sa fermeté;" *ston-pa* with the terminative means "to show one's self as, to prove as, to furnish proof of being," etc. The word *brtan-po* or *brtan-pa* (also *rton-pa*, as in V. 23, *brton-pa*), with or without *yid*, means "to place confidence in a person" (JÄSCHKE, *Dictionary*, p. 215a); *brtan-po*, more specifically, refers to a permanency of condition in which a person continues to enjoy the confidence once obtained, while *brtan-pa* signifies a temporary action. It occurs in *Saddharmapundarīka*, where FOUCAUX (*Parabole de l'enfant égaré*, p. 54, Paris, 1854) renders it by "homme digne de confiance," and in *Bharatae responsa* (ed. SCHIEFNER, p. 46: *fidem habere*). The sense of this verse, accordingly, is, "(Le corbeau), en disant la vérité (ou, parce que ses augures sont véritables), se prouve digne de confiance."

V. 18. The two Tibetan expressions would theoretically correspond to Skr. *shaṭpaksha*, *shaṭparṇa*, but such Sanskrit terms do not exist. The whole idea apparently is not Indian. (M. BACOT's rendering, "six plumes devinrent six ailes," is not justified by the text, and yields no significance.) Here we must briefly touch on the religious ideas revealed by our text. Our knowledge of Tibetan folk-lore, and particularly of that of the past, is certainly still so scanty that for some time to come all speculations on such-like subjects must remain of a more or less tentative character. But with all their brevity, the twenty-nine verses of this Preface contain a good deal, and also, from the viewpoint of religious history, present a document of some importance. Above all, we notice that the ideas expressed by it are absent from the text of *Kākajariti*, and aptly fill the gap which we were obliged to point out there. It is the rôle of the Raven as a bird of divination which is here depicted. At first sight it is tempting to regard this description as breathing a certain Tibetan spirit. We know that the Raven plays a part in the sacred pantomimic dances of the Tibetan Lamas performed at the time of the New Year; he makes attempts at stealing the strewing oblation (*gtor-ma*), and is driven away with long sticks by two Atsara, skeleton ghouls, a skeleton being designed on their white cotton garbs, and their masks having the appearance of skulls. The mask of the Raven, though it is styled *bya-rog* by the Tibetans, has not at all the form of this bird, but that of the Indian Garuḍa, with big curved and hooked beak (while the raven's beak is straight). A specimen in the Field Museum, where are complete sets of Tibetan masks, shows the Raven's mask of dark-green color, with red bill, a blue eye of wisdom on his forehead, flamed eye-brows, and gold painted flames protruding from his jaws. The entire make-up is so unlike a raven, that the Chinese workman of Peking who manufactures the masks for the Lama temples of the capital styles it a parrot (*ying wu*). In the *Veda* the eagle carries off the *soma* or *amṛita* for Indra, and in the *Kāṭhaka* it is Indra himself who in the form of an eagle captures the beverage (A. A. MACDONELL, *Vedic Mythology*, p. 152; and H. OLDENBERG, *Die Religion des Veda*, p. 176). The *Mahābhārata* (*Āstikaparvan* XXXII) tells how Garuḍa, in order to take hold of the *amṛita*, defeats the host of the Deva, kills the guardians, and extinguishes the fire surrounding the *amṛita*. This Indian tradition seems to me in some way or other to be responsible for the cast of the Raven in the Tibetan sacred dances, and for certain elements of a sun-bird attached to the Raven in our text. The Indian source which has transmitted these ideas to Tibet certainly remains to be pointed out. If the raven was made the substitute of the Garuḍa in Tibet, this may be due to the world-wide reputation of that bird as a clever pilferer. The ancients regarded him as an all-round thief, particularly of sacrificial meat. In the sacred groves of Greece many ravens subsisted on the flesh which they seized from the altars and consumed in the trees (O. KELLER, *Die antike Tierwelt*, Vol. II, p. 93). The Kachin of Burma look upon the raven as the very first thief who subsequently was duly imitated by man (GILHODES, *Anthropos*, Vol. IV, 1909 p. 134).

On the other hand, the Tibetan mask of the Raven reminds us of the first of the seven degrees of initiation which the mystic successively assumed in the Mithraic cult, — the name of Raven (*corax*); the others being Occult, Soldier, Lion, Persian, Runner of the Sun, and Father (F. CUMONT, *The Mysteries of Mithra*, p. 152). CUMONT regards these as animal disguises going back to a prehistoric period when the deities themselves were represented under the forms of animals, and when the worshipper, in taking the name and semblance of his gods, believed that he identified himself with them. To the primitive titles of Raven and Lion others were afterward added for the purpose of attaining the sacred number seven, the seven degrees of initiation answering to the seven planetary spheres which the soul was forced to traverse in order to reach the abode of the blessed. It is in the Tibetan mystery-plays that we find the masks of the Raven and the Lion. In the belief of the Persians, the Raven was sacred to the God of Light and the Sun. On the Mithraic monuments he sits behind Mithras, sacrificing a bull, and, according to O. KELLER (*Die antike Tierwelt*, Vol. II, p. 104), the idea of the sacred Ravens assigned to Helios in Thessalia may have originated from Persia. The "six wings and six pinions" assigned in our text to the Raven in his quality as a bird of Heaven cannot be accounted for by any Indian notions, and it may well be doubted whether this feature is due to a creation of Tibetan mythology. It seems to me that also this trait savors of Mithraic elements, somehow inspired by the grotesque monsters of West-Asiatic imagination, particularly the winged griffins (see, for example, PERROT and CHIPIEZ, *History of Art in Persia*, Figs. 71, 72, 158, also 187; another Tibeto-Mithraic parallel is pointed out by GRÜNWEDEL, *Baessler-Archiv*, Vol. III, 1912, p. 15). The Persian influence on Tibetan religion is established, though it remains for the future to work up the details of the problem (GRÜNWEDEL, *Mythologie des Buddhismus*, p. 205, note 38). The historical foundation of the Bon religion of Tibet, as shown by me (*T'oung Pao*, 1908, p. 13), is Persian. The most significant feature revealed by this Preface, as already pointed out, is the Raven's function as the messenger of a god, so that his predictions appear as the expression of divine will. The Raven as a heavenly messenger is conscious of his presages. The same idea is expressed by PLINY (*Nat. Hist*, X, 12, § 32;

ed. MAYHOFF, Vol. II, p. 229): corvi in auspiciis soli videntur intellectum habere significationum suarum.

V. 19. M. BACOT renders this verse, "La terre des dieux arrive au ciel." He has apparently been led into error (the same matter occurs in V. 3, 6, 7, 11, 12, 18) by assuming that the particle *ni* distinguishes the subject of the sentence. This was the erroneous view of I. J. SCHMIDT, which was refuted by SCHIEFNER (*Mélanges asiatiques*, Vol. I, p. 384). *Ni* is simply an emphatic particle added to any word or group of words in order to single them out (JÄSCHKE, *Tibetan Grammar*, p. 66). It may follow any adverb and any phrase expressing space or time, the genitive, dative, instrumentalis, or locative; and in metrical composition, it may take any place where a syllable is to be filled in (a peculiar case not discussed in our grammars is *na ni* forming the unreal conditional sentence). There are assuredly numerous cases where stress is laid upon the subject by the addition of this particle, then corresponding in meaning to Japanese *wa* and *ga;* but this rule must not be turned into the opposite, that wherever *ni* is employed, the subject is hinted at. Our text is very instructive as to the application of *ni*, since in each verse it occurs in the third syllable with intentional regularity, and lends to the style a somewhat oracular tinge. First of all, it is employed because of the metre to produce a dactyl in the first foot of each verse; simultaneously, certain words, as *p'o-rog* and *dran-sron* in V. 1 and 2, are singled out with strong emphasis by its presence. In V. 4, 10, 11, 16, 21, 23, it is entirely superfluous and merely a rhythmic factor. As to V. 3 and 19, we should have *na* in its place in a prose text, in V. 9 *nas*, in V. 18 *dan*. If the author should have pinned his faith to a purely trochaic metre, which is the most frequent in Tibetan, he could easily have accomplished his purpose by dropping all the *ni*, and yet the sense of his words would have remained exactly the same.

V. 22. M. BACOT renders this verse, "Homme et raison ne font pas un." Whatever this may mean, it is evident that the Tibetan people do not indulge in metaphysical speculations of that sort, and that such a sentence has no *raison d'être* in this context. We notice that this text is a plain account of the Raven as a bird of augury, and that everything logically refers to it in a palpably concrete manner. For this reason we are justified in seeking the interpretation of the verb *rtog-pa* in the same direction. We met it in the Tibetan title of the *Kākajariti*, where it is used in regard to the "examination" of the sounds or cries of the crow, and I believe it is here used in exactly the same sense. The word *myi* preceding it is in parallel opposition to *lhai* of the previous verse, and, like the latter, may be construed as a genitive ("examination of the auguries on the part of man") or in the sense of a dative depending on *mo'is* ("to man . . . there is"). The particle *ma* can, of course, be looked upon as the negation, as M. Bacot considers it, but this does not make sense. I prefer to read *gcig-ma*, "unity, oneness," (regarding *-ma* with words denoting space, time, etc. see Schiefner, *Mélanges asiatiques*, Vol. I, pp. 385, 386), and understand the verse to the effect that there is for man only one and the same method of examining the forebodings of the Raven, that is, the method laid down in the Table. This interpretation seems to be in keeping with the spirit of the text. If the Raven is a heavenly bird, a messenger of the gods, and the herald of their commands, if he is truthful and trustworthy, it is logical that there should be but one way of studying and interpreting his notes. The comment furnished by the Lama is quite in harmony with this point of view. He likewise understands the words *gcig ma mc'is* in a positive sense by transcribing them *gcig ạdra byed*, "make like one, might be one;" and his note *mi t'ams-cad rtog-pa ni* sufficiently indicates that these words mean an examination referring to all men, and that *rtog-pa* is not intended for *rtogs-pa*, "knowledge, perception." The copula *mc'is* belongs to the *estilo culto*.

Analogous examples for the use of *gcig-ma* are *rkaṅ gcig-ma* "one-footed," *rkaṅ gñis-ma* "two-footed" (Schiefner, *Mélanges asiatiques*, Vol. III, p. 12); *ral gcig-ma* = Skr. *ekajaṭā* (P. Cordier, *l. c.*, pp. 122, 194, 195); *skad cig-ma* "a moment," *skad gcig-ma* "instantaneousness" (in the philosophy of the Sautrāntika: Vasilyev, *Der Buddhismus*, p. 305); and *skad cig-ma-ñid*, "the short (instantaneous) duration of life" (in the commentary of *Suhṛil-lekha*). The title of a small treatise describing the offerings to Vajrabhairava is *drug bcu-pa-ma*. The title *ratnamālā* is once translated in the Tanjur *rin c'en p'reṅ-ba-ma* (usually *p'reṅ-ba*), where *ma* is to express the feminine gender of Sanskrit; and so it may be concluded that the influence of Sanskrit is responsible also for the other cases of this kind.

V. 23. M. Bacot translates, "Croyance et confiance de l'esprit font un." This is in contradiction to an elementary rule of Tibetan grammar. The final *cig* does not mean "one," but is the well-known sign of the imperative; besides, the form *rton* is an imperative in itself (from *rten-pa*), and also the Lama has plainly indicated another imperative form, *t'ob cig*. The phrase *sems rten* (*rton*) in this passage corroborates the interpretation given for *brtan-po* in V. 16. *Yid c'es* may be taken as *adverbialis* ("with faith, faithfully"), or as a verb to be supplemented by the following *cig* ("have faith and" ...). The Lama explains this faith as "prayer to the gods" (*lha-la gsol*), which is hardly necessary. Both faith and confidence, first of all, refer to the Raven and his auguries, as presented in the Table; and faith in him naturally implies faith in the gods who sent him.

V. 27. In Table IV, 1, M. Bacot translates the sentence *riṅs-pa žig oṅ-bar slon* by "indique qu'une personne vient en hâte." But *riṅs-pa žig* is the subject of the sentence, and means "a distant one, a person coming from a distance." True it is, *riṅs-pa* means also "swift, speedy." The spelling, however, must never lead us astray: it is here intended for *riṅ-ba*, meaning "distant" as to space and time, hence "long" (the K'ien-lung Polyglot Dictionary confronts it with *yüan* 遠 and Manchu *goro*). The word *riṅs-par* in V. 27, in my opinion, contains an allusion to the passage of the Table quoted. M. Bacot's translation, "est signe de rapidité," has no meaning. Also the Lama is on my side when he interprets *mi yoṅ*, "a man will come." — Compare *Subāshitaratnanidhi* 66 (ed. Csoma, *J. A. S. B.*, Vol. VII, 1912, Extra No., p. 116): *rin c'en gliṅ-du riṅ-nas ạdu*, "they flock from a distance to the Island of Jewels."

V. 28. The foretelling of the arrival of a friend, in all likelihood, is fraught with a deeper significance than may appear on the surface. In the Table (VIII, 6; and X, 3) we find twice the prophecy of a meeting with a great friend. The word used in each case is *grog*, which is pronounced and written also *rog*, *rogs*. Now, the Tibetans, for this reason, pun the word (*bya-*)*rog*, "raven" with *rog*, *grog*, "friend." An excellent example of this fact is furnished by the interesting little work *Bya c'os rin c'en ạp'reṅ-ba*, "The Precious Wreath (*ratnamālā*) of the Teachings of Birds," the text of which has been edited by S. Chandra Vidyabhusan under the title *Bya-Chos or the Religion of Birds: being an Old Tibetan Story*, Calcutta, 1903 (40 p.). Jäschke (*Dictionary*, p. 372) mentions this graceful work, styling it also *Bya skad*, "Bird Voices," or *Bya sgruṅs*, "Bird Stories," and characterizing it as a book of satirical fables, in which birds are introduced as speaking. I am under the impression that no satire is veiled under this text, at least not in the edition quoted, and that it belongs to the class of Nītiçāstra, as indicated by its very title. In order to teach the birds the tenets of the Buddhist doctrine, Avalokiteçvara transforms himself into the king of the birds, the large cuckoo (*kokila*), and finally attracts the attention of the other birds by his meditation carried on for many years in a sandal-tree. The birds congregate around him, and each recites in its language a number of stanzas in praise or support of Buddhist ethical teachings (compare *Mantic Uttair ou le langage des oiseaux*, poème de philosophie religieuse traduit du persan de Farid Uddin Attar par M. Garcin de Tassy, Paris, 1863, and the same author's *La poésie philosophique et religieuse chez les Persans d'après le Mantic Uttair*, Paris, 1864; this Persian work has doubtless received its impetus from that genre of Buddhist literature, as I hope to demonstrate in a future translation of the Tibetan book). The *Bya c'os* is not a translation from Sanskrit, but a witty Tibetan production, though fundamentally based on Indian thought; it is full of fun and pun. The verses recited by the birds terminate in a refrain, and this refrain consists of a catchword forming a pun upon the name of the particular bird. The snipe (*tiṅ-tiṅ-ma*), for instance, puns upon *gtiṅ riṅ*, "a deep abyss," in this style: "The ocean of the misery of Saṁsāra is a deep abyss, the hell of Māra is a deep abyss," etc. Or the jack-daw (*skyuṅ-ka*) puns upon the verb *skyuṅ-ba*, "to leave behind;" the owl (*ug-pa*), on *u-sdug* (= *u-tʻug*), "destitute;" the ptarmigan (*goṅ-mo*), on *go-dka*, "difficult to understand." And the watchword of the raven (*pʻo-rog*) is *grogs yoṅ grogs yoṅ*, "a friend will come, a friend will come," exactly as in the above verse of the *document Pelliot*. In this case, the coming of the friend is interpreted in the figurative sense of Buddhist blessings. The Raven speaks thus:

"When moral obligations have been fulfilled, happiness will come as a friend.

"When alms have been distributed, wealth will come in the future as a friend.

"When religious functions have been performed, thy tutelary deity will come as a friend.

"When the vows are pure, the delight of heaven will come as a friend.

"When the sacrificial feast was vigorous, the Protector of Religion (*dharmapāla*) will come as a friend.

"When thy achievements correspond to the length of thy life, Buddha, in the future, will come as a friend.

"This *siddhi* of 'the friend who will come' take to heart and keep in mind!"

The coming of the friend appears also in *K.* (I, south; III, north), and from the viewpoint of Sanskrit, a play upon words can hardly be intended. We might therefore infer that simply the transmission of this Indian idea gave rise in Tibet to the formation of the quibble "raven — friend," which is apparent in *Bya cʻos* (compare also the identical formations *,a-rog*, "friend," and *,o-rog*, "raven"). The date of this work is unfortunately unknown; the mention of the Siddha Saraha in the introduction, in a measure, may yield a *terminus a quo*. At any rate, *Bya cʻos* is far posterior to *K.* and *document Pelliot*. Does the prophecy *grog yoṅ* in the latter imply an allusion to the name of the raven? The case would be interesting from a philological point of view; if the allusion could be established as a positive fact, it would prove that the word *grog* was sounded *rog* as early as the ninth century, for only under this condition is the *bon mot* possible; or another possibility would be that the two forms *grog* and *rog* co-existed at that time. At any rate, there is in our text an obvious relation between the sound *krog krog* and the word *grog*, accordingly a divination founded on punning (*krog krog* is a recognized word of the language and recorded as such in *Za-ma-tog: Studien zur Sprachwissenschaft der Tibeter*, p. 574). This etymological kind of augury finds an interesting analogy among the Arabs, among whom the appearance of a raven indicates parting or pilgrimage, as the word for raven comes from a root meaning "to be a stranger;" the name for the hoopoe suggests "guidance," whence its appearance is of good omen to the wanderer (HASTINGS, *Encyclopaedia of Religion*, Vol. IV, p. 816). Among birds, the ancient Arabic poets most frequently mention a black and white spotted species of crow and a black one which it is disastrous to scare, and whose croaking signifies separation from a mistress (G. Jacob, *Altarabisches Beduinenleben*, p. 22, Berlin, 1897). Another explanation than the above is given by D. C. Phillott (*Note on the Common Raven*, *J. A. S. B.*, N. S., Vol. III, 1908, p. 115); the Arabs, according to him, call the raven "raven of separation," because it separated itself from Noah and failed to return. This bird of ill omen alights on the deserted habitations of men; it mourns like one afflicted; when it sees friends together, it croaks, and its croaking foretells "separation;" and when it sees well-peopled habitations, it announces their ruin and desolation. If it croaks thrice, the omen is evil; but if twice, it is good. Possibly the two explanations exist side by side. — Similar etymological punning in augury takes place in Annam with reference to the bird *khéo*. "Le mot *khách*, étranger, devient par corruption patoise, *khéc*, comme le nom de l'oiseau. De là un jeu de mots sur le nom de l'oiseau: Si le *khéc* crie à la porte d'entrée, c'est signe de l'arrivée de visiteurs venant de loin: s'il crie derrière la maison, ce sont des parents qui vont arriver" (L. Cadière, *B. E. F. E. O.*, Vol. I, 1901, p. 196).

V. 29. M. Bacot translates "est signe d'intermédiaire." I do not believe that this is the sense intended, as omens of middle quality (*ạbriṅ*) are referred to in V. 26. The Lama understands that "the sound ,*iu* ,*iu* is continually his (the raven's) note." It is not intelligible to me how he arrives at this view of the matter. The phrase *bar ston* is somewhat embarrassing. I should be inclined to construe *bar* as an abbreviation of *bar-c'ad*, "accident, calamity," and as referring to the prophecy of calamities given in *K.*, where this word is used; but the fact remains that it does not occur in our Table, and it is certainly to this our Table that we have to look for the interpretation of the term, as in the two preceding verses. There we observe that the greater number of oracles close with the words *oṅ bar ston*, and that in fact each of the ninety oracles ends in the two syllables *bar ston*, or, what is practically the same, *par ston*. This typical formula, I believe, should be recognized in the *bar ston* of V. 29, which accordingly means that the sound ,*iu* ,*iu* points to any of the ninety oracles enumerated in the Table, and therewith the Preface is happily closed with a direct appeal to the latter. This conception of the matter is satisfactory also from a grammatical point of view; for *bar* in this case is *ba* + *r*, and the terminative is required in connection with *ston*, as shown by V. 25—27 and the ninety examples of the Table, while *bar* taken in the sense of "intermediate, middle," would be the formless *casus indefinitus*, and decidedly present a grammatical anomaly.

## Palæographic Traits.

The plain consonant, according to the rules of Tibeto-Indian writing, implies the vowel *a*. In seven cases we find an additional letter *a* following a consonant in this document, where no *a* is admissible in modern writing. The word *dgra* is four times written this way (Table II, 9; IV, 4; V, 2; VIII, 8); further, the suffix *pa* in V. 18, *blta* in V. 11, and *bya* in V. 14. Mr. Barnett (in A. Stein, *Ancient Khotan*, Vol. I, p. 549) has made a similar observation in the fragments of the *Çālistambasūtra*. He says that before a short pause a final *a* sometimes appears to be lengthened to *ā*, the letter *a* being added on the line; and on p. 500 he adds in a note that this lengthening seems due to the short pause following. I regret being unable to share this opinion; I can see no reason (and Mr. Barnett gives none) why this addition of *a* should indicate a lengthening of the vowel. True it is, a subjoined *a* (the so-called *a ạdogs*) denotes *ā* in the Tibetan transcription of Sanskrit words; and it may even be granted with reserve that in the word *gso* (p. 553, note 6), as Mr. Barnett is inclined to think, the subjoined letter *a* may be intended to give the phonetic value of long *ō*.[1]) But there must be some difference between *a* written beneath and *a* written alongside a consonant. Why, if the lengthening of the vowel is intended, is the letter *a* not subscribed too in the other

1) An analogous case is known to me in the Tibetan version of the *Jātakamālā*, a print of 1430, where (vol. II, fol. 9) the word *rgya-mts'o* is equipped with an additional letter *a* under the letter *ts'*. — The subscribed letter *a* occurs also in Tibetan transcriptions of Chinese words; and it would be wrong to conclude, that, because it denotes length in Sanskrit words, it does so also in the case of Chinese, which has no long vowels. In the Tibetan inscription of 822, line 15 (see plate in Bushell, *The Early History of Tibet*), we have Tib. *bun bu* (each with subjoined *a*) as transcriptions of Chin. 文武 *wên wu* (Japanese *bun bu*). Most certainly, the additional *a* was not intended by the Tibetans to express a Chinese *ū*, but a peculiar Chinese timbre of *u*, which was not sufficiently reproduced by the plain Tibetan *u*.

cases mentioned? The further question arises, If the ancient Tibetan language should have made a clear distinction between short and long *a*, and if an attempt at discrimination between the two in writing should have been contemplated, why is this distinction not carried through with regular and convincing persistency? Why does it only appear in a few isolated cases? And if this project were once set on foot, how could it happen that it was dropped so soon, as not a trace of it has survived in later literature? Considerations like these should render us cautious in accepting the view of Mr. Barnett. It is highly improbable that long *ā* (and in general long vowels) existed in Tibetan. It seems to me that long vowels are in Tibetan merely of secondary origin, being the outcome of a fusion of two joining vowels, or arising from the elision of final consonants.[1]) In our text we notice that the word *bya*,

1) Jäschke (*Tibetan Grammar*, p. 4), who assuredly possessed a good ear, expressly states, "It ought to be specially remarked that all vowels, including *e* and *o* (unlike the Sanskrit vowels from which they have taken their signs) are short, since no long vowels at all occur in the Tibetan language, except under particular circumstances mentioned below." Compare the same author's *Ueber die Phonetik der tibetischen Sprache* (*Monatsberichte Berliner Akademie*, 1866, p. 152). For the same reason I am unable to share the opinion of Mr. Waddell (*J. R. A. S.*, 1909, p. 945) when he tries to make out short and long *i* in the Tibetan inscription of A. D. 783. The short *i* following its Indian Devanāgarī prototype, according to Mr. Waddell, is represented there by a reversion of the tail of the superposed sign to the left, which is not found in modern Tibetan manuscripts. But what evidence is there that the letter *i* with tail to the left should denote in Tibetan a short, and *ī* with tail to the right a long vowel? This is an arbitrary and unfounded opinion. Why should — taking the examples from the text of the inscription as transcribed by Mr. Waddell — *gyi, kyi, srid, myi, ni, yin, riṅ, k'rims, ḍdi*, etc., have a short *i*, but *bris, šiṅ, gcig* (*gtsig* in line 2 is a misprint), *dgyis, žiṅ, bkris, bži, ciṅ, ži-ba, k'rim, drin, p'yin, p'rin, rṅiṅ, lci*, etc., have a long *ī*, — words which at present are all pronounced with the vowel short? There are, further, several inconsistencies due either to the original or to Mr. Waddell's transcript. The interrogative pronoun *cī* has the long vowel in line 3, the short vowel in line 45; the particle of the genitive *kyi*, otherwise short, becomes long in line 68; *rṅiṅ* is long in line 55, but short in line 66; -*ī*, the sign of the genitive, is usually long, but short in line 60. The author remarks that the distinction of the short *i* by reversal of the superscribed limb has not been noted in every instance. On p. 1276, where two other inscriptions are transcribed, he says, "In this copy

"bird," is followed by the letter *a* in but a single case (V. 14), while in two other cases (V. 8 and 17) it is written without it. Why should it be *byā* in the one, and *byă* in the two other cases? In fact, however, the vowel of *bya* is not long, but short or quite indeterminate in regard to length. Nor can it be argued with Mr. BARNETT that the juxtaposition of *a* and the alleged vocalic lengthening are due to the pause, for we have *bya* + *a* at the close of V. 14, and *bya* without *a* at the close of V. 17. Now, what is

---

the distinction between the long and short *i* has not been recorded." An important palaeographic and phonetic fact is revealed by these inscriptions: in the one case it is dealt with in a perfectly arbitrary manner, as suits the author's convenience; in the other case it is simply suppressed. This is a singular method of editing texts. The student who is desirous of investigating this phenomenon will therefore turn away from these artifacts and for the time being have recourse to the facsimile reproduction of the Tibeto-Chinese inscription of A. D. 822 appended to Dr. BUSHELL's *Early History of Tibet*, where the same distinction of the two *i*'s occurs. The inscriptions published by Mr. WADDELL, for this and several other reasons, will have to be studied anew in the future, on the basis of facsimile rubbings actually taken from the stones. In regard to this peculiar form of *i*, Mr. WADDELL is wrong in asserting that it is not found in modern Tibetan manuscripts. It occurs in all good manuscripts and prints denoting the vocalic *ṛ* and *ḷ* of Sanskrit words, as may be seen, for example, in pl. I of CHANDRA DAS, *The Sacred and Ornamental Characters of Tibet* (*J. A. S. B.*, Vol. LVII, pt. 1, 1888); and this is the only positive fact which we thus far know about the meaning of this sign in Tibetan. It is frequently employed in *P'yi rabs mi-la bslab bya*, a manuscript of the India Office Library alluded to by SCHIEFNER (*Mélanges asiatiques*, Vol. VIII, p. 624), in words as *mi*, *yin*, *p'yis*, *k'ri*, *ḍdi*, and in the particles of the genitive *kyi* and *-i*, but with no apparent regularity. The sign, further, occurs in the rock-carved inscriptions of Ladākh published by A. H. FRANCKE (*Indian Antiquary*, Vol. XXXII, 1903, pp. 361—363, pl. VIII); there we meet it in the endings of the genitive, *gi* and *-i*, which proves how unfounded Waddell's opinion is, for the supposition that the genitive sign *-i* should be short in Ladākh and long in Central Tibet would be absurd. The distinction of the two *i*'s, in my opinion, does not relate to quantity, which did not exist, but was made to express two different phonetic values or timbres of *i*, which are determined farther on. The vowel system of Tibetan, also at the time of the introduction of writing, was far richer than it appears from the five main vowels *a*, *e*, *i*, *o*, *u*, the only ones expressed in writing; and for a certain length of time an attempt at discriminating between two values of *i* seems to have been made. — The inverted sign *i* is still employed also, for typographical reasons, in cases where there is no space for the ordinary vowel-sign; as occurs, for instance, when in the line above a word with the vowel-sign *u* (especially the combinations *-yu*, *-ru* hanging beneath the line proper) is printed.

the rule? Our material is certainly still too scanty to admit of positive conclusions. We have to wait till more ancient documents turn up. Meanwhile it is incumbent upon us to record all peculiarities *le cas échéant,* and to beware of premature and generalized judgments, which will do more harm than good to the future student, and which may be exploded at any moment by the reading of a new document. A conclusion as to the existence of long and short vowels in ancient Tibetan is certainly a case of importance, not only for Tibetan but also for Indo-Chinese philology, as the latter is vitally affected by the former; but such a case must be founded on facts, not on guesswork. Basing my opinion on the *document Pelliot,* I am under the impression that the addition of the letter *a* is not charged with a phonetic value, but has a mere graphic function. The writing of such words as *dgra* and *blta* with an additional *a* moves along the same line as words like *dga, bka, mk'a, dma,* etc., where the vowel *a* is still expressed by the presence of the letter *a* to avoid ambiguity, as without it the readings *dag, bak, dam,* would be possible (CSOMA, *Grammar of the Tibetan Language,* p. 17). Writing was then in its initial stage; and the rule as to when the letter *a* was a necessity, and when it could be dispensed with, was not yet clearly developed. To all appearances it was then granted a wider latitude; and for the sake of greater distinctness, the *a* was rather added than omitted. In other cases it is neglected where it is demanded by modern rule: thus, in the *Çālistambasūtra,* the word *mk'a* is once expressed by the two letters *mk'* (*Ancient Khotan,* p. 552, D 9). One point is clear, that at the time when, and in those localities where, the *da drag* was still in vogue, the rule necessarily had to meet a more extensive application; for there the word *brda,* for instance, if unaccompanied by the letter *a,* could have as well been read *bard.* As this word is written *bda* in our text, it was certainly necessary to add the letter *a*; but it is just this word *brda* which even in modern prints is spelled with *a* as well as without it; the spelling with *a* is, for example, the rule in K'ien-lung's *Dictionary in Four Languages.* If it should turn out through further investigations that this *a* occurs with special predilection in the suffixes *pa*, *ba*, etc., at the end of a sentence, it may very well be that it is a graphic sign employed to mark a certain stress or emphasis, or to denote a stop.

Our text is characterized by two negative features, — the absence of the final *o*, which may be explained by the fact that this text is written in colloquial style, whereas the final *o* is restricted to the written language; [1]) and the lack of the so-called *da drag*.

---

1) It is in full swing in the Stein fragments of the *Çālistambasūtra* and in the sgraffiti of Endere, as well as in the ancient inscriptions of Lhasa, — all documents of the written language. The origin and meaning of this final *o* have not yet been explained. A. CSOMA (*Grammar of the Tibetan Language*, p. 84) has merely noticed the fact. When FOUCAUX (*Grammaire de la langue tibétaine*, p. 17) observes that the particle *o* has the signification of the verbs "to be, to have, to make," this is only to the point in that the sentence, in some instances, may thus be translated by us, but it is not correct from a Tibetan viewpoint. From JÄSCHKE (*Tibetan Grammar*, p. 45) it only appears that the principal verb of a sentence closing it receives in written Tibetan in most cases the mark *o*, by which the end of a period may be known. This *o*, in my opinion, is identical with the now antiquated demonstrative pronoun *o* (compare Lepcha *o-re*) which, according to SCHIEFNER (*Ergänzungen*, etc., p. 49), very rarely occurs. He points out *padma o-ni*, "this lotus," in the Kanjur (Vol. 74, fol. 46), and *groṅ-k'yer o-nir ạgro*, "to go into that town," in *ạDsaṅs-blun* (compare also *Mélanges asiatiques*, Vol. I, p. 385; and *Ueber Pluralbezeichnungen*, *l. c.*, §§ 21, 22). In the Tibetan prose version of *Avadānakalpalatā* (p. 262, line 20) we find, *k'yed ni . . . lus so šiṅ bžin skam-pa aṅ srid*, "this your body seems to be dried up like wood;" and (p. 184, line 19), *o ri-dvags gser-logs ạdi-o žes*, "this one here is that gazelle gSer-logs by name." The latter example is very instructive in showing the pronoun *o* preceding a noun, and again at the end of the sentence linked to the related pronoun *ạdi*, *ạdi-o* apparently meaning "this is." The frequent phrase *o-na*, abbreviated into *on*, embodies a survival of this pronoun, the literal meaning being "if this is so." The pronoun *o* itself represents the remains of the entire vowel series which must have originally had pronominal significance. In Ladākhi (A. H. FRANCKE, *Sketch of Ladakhi Grammar*, p. 28, Calcutta, 1901) we have *i* or *i-bo*, "this," and *a* or *a-bo*, "that." In eastern Tibet we have *e*, for example *e-de mi*, "that man" (beside *o-de*; A. DESGODINS, *Essai de grammaire thibétaine*, p. 39, Hongkong, 1899), and in Tsang and Sikkim *u-di* (JÄSCHKE, *Dictionary*, p. 499, and G. SANDBERG, p. 85; also according to the writer's own observation), with the survival *u-nir*, *o-nir*, "hither," in the written language. Also the

This term means "strong *d*" or "strengthening *d*." A. Csoma was already acquainted with the occurrence of this phenomenon in ancient orthography, as shown by the spellings *stond-ka, dbyard-ka, rgyald-ka* (*Grammar of the Tibetan Language*, p. 28); *gsand-tam, k'yerd-tam, gsold-tam* (p. 29); *gsand-to, gyurd-to, gsold-to* (p. 30), and his note on p. 11. Foucaux (*Grammaire de la langue tibétaine*, p. 14), in accordance with Csoma, speaks of three ancient double affixes, — *nd* or *nt*, *rd* or *rt*, *ld* or *lt* (the *d* was evidently pronounced with *auslautschärfung*, as the final media in many modern dialects), — and adds that this *d* is now omitted, and that probably, under the influence of this ancient spelling, *gyur-to, gyur-tam, zin-to*, are still written. The terminations *to* and *tam* cannot be considered as survivals; for the dental is nothing but the very *da drag* itself, the terminations proper being *o* (see the note below) and *am*. It is therefore wrong to say that the *da drag* is obsolete: it is obsolete only as a graphic element, in that it is no longer actually written;

---

personal pronouns *u-cag, u-bu-cag, o-cag, o-skol*, etc. must be explained from this demonstrative pronoun. In the same manner, there was extant in a primeval period of the language a complete vowel series in the *d* group of the demonstrative pronoun, of which only *ạdi* and *de* have survived. But we have such remnants as *da nañ* and *da rañs*, "this morning;" *da lo*, "this year;" *do nub*, "this evening;" *do gdoñ*, "to-night;" *do žag* or *do mod*, "to-day," — examples in which *da* and *do* doubtless have the function of a demonstrative pronoun. — The Tibetan verb is, strictly speaking, a verbal noun, which for this reason could easily be connected with a demonstrative pronoun: the sentence *ṅas mt'oñ-ṅo* literally means "by me this seeing (is done)." The fact that this final *o* is not a verbal particle proper follows from its association with any word category; it may be joined to a noun, an adjective, a pronoun, a numeral, the original function of the demonstrative pronoun still being in prominence, with the significance of a completed action or description (hence the Tibetan name for this final is *rdsogs ts'ig*, "word of completion," while its other designation, *slar bsdu-ba*, refers to its position at the end of the sentence). There is, for instance, *bstan bcos ạgyur-r-o-cog* (Laufer, *Dokumente*, I, p. 49), and such combinations appear as subject or object within a sentence; compare *gsol-l-o mc'od-d-o sruñ skyobs mdsod* (A. H. Francke, *Der Wintermythus der Kesarsage*, p. 9), "guard these prayers and these offerings!" (where Francke, p. 66, comments that "the termination *o* is here inexplicable, unless it may have arisen from the emphatic articles *bo, po*"). — It is noteworthy that at the conclusion of the Preface we find, not *ston-no*, but the popular *ston yin*.

but it is fully alive phonetically, as soon as certain affixes, to which also *ciṅ*, *ces*, and *cig* belong (*Studien zur Sprachwissenschaft der Tibeter*, *Sitzungsberichte der bayerischen Akad.*, 1898, p. 584), are joined to the word. We are easily deceived by the appearance of writing. In the Tibetan alphabet is developed the principle of writing separately each syllable of a word and of any composite formation; this, however, does not mean at all that what is separated by the use of the syllabic dot in writing presents also an independent part phonetically. If dissyllabic words, as *me-tog*, *me-loṅ*, *mu-ge*, *p'o-ña*, *t'a-ga(-pa)*, are written in two syllables for the mere reason that the monosyllable is the basic principle of Tibetan writing, it does not follow that these words are compounds; on the contrary, they are stem words consisting of two syllables, and should phonetically be written *metog*, *meloṅ*, *muge*, *p'oña*, *t'aga* (from *t'ag*, "to weave"). In the same manner we find *rdsogs-so* written in two syllables, and *rdsogso* written in one graphic syllable; the pronunciation is not *rdsogs so*, but *rdsogs-o*. In other words, this is not a case of phonetic, but merely of graphic reduplication, caused by the principle of writing. Likewise it does not make any difference from a phonetic viewpoint whether the Tibetan spells *gyurd-to* or *gyur-to*; phonetically it is neither the one nor the other, but *gyurt-o*. Consequently the rule as expressed by JÄSCHKE (*Tibetan Grammar*, p. 45, and *Dictionary*, p. 246) — "*da drag* is a term used by grammarians for the now obsolete *d* as second final, after *n*, *r*, *l*, *e. g.* in *kund*, changing the termination *du* into *tu*; *no*, *ro*, *lo* into *to*; *nam*, *ram*, *lam* into *tam*" — is, from a scientific standpoint, wrong. The rule ought to be formulated that a number of stems at present terminating in *n*, *r*, *l*, were formerly capable of assuming a final *d* sharpened into *t*, and quite regularly assumed the terminations *-u*, *-o*, and *-am*; of course, the proper form of the particle denoting the terminative is *-u*, and not *ru*, *tu*, *du*, *su*, as our grammars merely state for practical purposes, the consonants *r*, *t*, and *d* being inserted for euphonic reasons, and *su* joined to a word with final *s* being solely a graphic picture of no phonetic value (*e.g.*, *nags-su* of writing = *nags-u* phonetically). The presence of the *da drag* was known to us for a long time only through the medium of the native grammarians, till Mr. BARNETT (*J. R. A. S.*, 1903, p. 110, and *Ancient Khotan*, Vol. I, p. 549) found it written in a large number of cases in the Stein fragments of *Çālistambasūtra*. But, Mr. BARNETT observes, "in isolated instances it is omitted in our MS. from roots that elsewhere have it, a fact indicating that it was already beginning to be dropped in actual speech." This is a point which I venture to challenge. Spelling and speech are in Tibetan two matters distinct; and, as shown above, spelling is not a true mirror of the phonetic state in the present case. The vacillating spelling in the *Çālistambasūtra* simply proves that there was no hard and fast rule for the application of this *d* in writing; but it does not at all prove that if or because it was not written, it was not sounded, at least in many cases.[1]) In other cases when it was omitted, there was surely no necessity for it; and the problem, after all, amounts to this, — What is the significance of this additional *d*? This question is raised neither by Mr. BARNETT, nor by Mr. A. H. FRANCKE (*Ancient Khotan*, p. 564), nor by Mr. WADDELL (*J. R. A. S.*, 1909,

---

1) There is a practical example in our Preface from which it may be demonstrated that the *da drag*, though not fixed in writing, nevertheless may have been sounded (see note on p. 61). Further, Mr. Barnett may be refuted with examples furnished by his own text. In D 3 (p. 551) occurs the writing *rkyen ạdi*, and in the next line *rkyend ạdi*. Now, should this indicate two different pronunciations co-existing at that time? Certainly not. The pronunciation simply was *rkyendi* in either case. The two spellings solely indicate two modes of writing these words in that period; they could be written either way, say, for instance, in the same manner as we have the two systems of Webster and Worcester in English spelling, and the latter days' questionable boon of simplified spelling.

pp. 942, 1250), who notes the absence of *da drag* in the inscription of A. D. 783 and its occurrence in another inscription from the first part of the ninth century. The latter document, according to Mr. WADDELL, retained the old popular [why popular?] style of orthography, while it is lacking in the older inscription, because it was revised by the staff of scholarly Indian and Tibetan monks working under the orders of King K'ri-sroṅ lde-btsan [there is no evidence for such a statement]. The *document Pelliot* is highly popular and even written in the language of the people, and shows no trace of the writing of a *da drag*. The whole argumentation of Mr. Waddell, owing to its subjective character, is not convincing; [1]) and it is difficult to see how anybody could argue out this case with any chance of success, without previously examining what a *da drag* is.

First, we have to note that the application of this sign is not quite so obsolete as heretofore stated. It is upheld, no doubt under the force of tradition, in many manuscripts; I observed it repeatedly, for instance, in eighteenth century gold and silver written manuscripts of the *Ashṭasāhasrikāprajñāpāramitā* with the Tibetan title *šes-rab-kyi p'a rold tu p'yin-pa.* The mere occurrence of a *da drag* is therefore no absolute valid proof for the antiquity of a

1) On this occasion Mr. WADDELL remarks that the *drag* "has always [?] been recognized by the English lexicographers of Tibetan as a genuine archaism." The English lexicographers of Tibetan! — I regret that they are unknown to me. The first Tibetan dictionary edited by SCHRÖTER (Serampore, 1826) is based on the materials of a Roman Catholic missionary, Father Juvenal (see *The Academy*, 1893, pp. 465, 590; Father FELIX, *J. A. S. B.*, Vol. VIII, 1912, p. 385, without knowledge of this article, attributes the materials of this dictionary to Orazio della Penna). Csoma, as known to everybody, was a Hungarian. I. J. Schmidt, A. Schiefner, H. A. Jäschke, were Germans. Vasilyov, to whom also Tibetan lexicography owes much, was a Russian. "Les missionnaires catholiques du Thibet," figuring as the authors on the title-page of the Tibetan-Latin-French Dictionary published at Hongkong in 1899, were assuredly not Englishmen; and Sarat Chandra Das is a Bengāli. Or does Mr. Waddell's philosophy include every English-speaking or English-writing person in the category of Englishmen?

manuscript; nor does its suppression constitute evidence against antiquity, as demonstrated by the *document Pelliot* and the inscription of 783. Secondly, we have to consult the Tibetan grammarians, and to study what they know anent the subject. The most complete native grammar is *Si-tui sum-rtags*, edited in 1743 by gTsug-lag c$^c$os-kyi snañ-ba of Si-tu in the province of K$^c$ams, and reprinted by the Bengal Secretariat Press in 1895.[1]) In this work, grammatical rules are illustrated by numerous examples, and the *da drag*, wherever applicable, is strictly maintained. Thus we meet on p. 19 the forms *kund-tu, p$^c$a-rold-tu, mts$^c$ard-tu, ạdsind-la*, [2]) *ạdsind-na, ạdserd-la, ạdserd-na, stsald-la, stsald-na*; on p. 24, *ạbreld*; on p. 30, *bstand kyañ, ạbyord kyañ, stsald kyañ*; on p. 33, *gyurd tam, ạts$^c$ald tam*; on p. 102, *bstand, bkand, bkard, bstard, bcald, mnand, bgard, bsald, mk$^c$yend, mts$^c$ard, ạk$^c$ruld, ạdund byed, ạdserd byed, gsold byed, mt$^c$ard byed, ạp$^c$end byed, bstund bžin-pa, gsold bžin-pa*, etc., but *gnon bžin-pa, gtor bžin-pa*; on p. 103, *rtsald, rold; sbrand, zind, smind, byind, p$^c$yind, t$^c$ard, ts$^c$ard*, but *dul, šar, bor, ts$^c$or, t$^c$al*, further *stond, stend, rtend, sbyind, skurd, spruld, speld, lend, smond, seld, ñand*, but *sgrun, snron, sgyur, k$^c$ur*; on p. 108, *stond-ka* ('autumn'), *berd-ka* ('staff'), *mk$^c$yend-pa, p$^c$and-pa, p$^c$yind-pa, stond-pa*; and on p. 110, *dkond-cog, rind-c$^c$en, lhand cig*. On pp. 15 and 16 the part played by this *d* is explained

---

1) This work is mentioned by A. Csoma, *Enumeration of Historical and Grammatical Works to be met with in Tibet* (*J. A. S. B.*, Vol. VII, 1838, p. 152); but Situ or lDom-bu-pa are not the names of the author, as stated by Csoma, but merely titles. He is styled "the great Paṇḍita of Situ" (compare *Si-tui sum rtags*, p. 187, and Chandra Das, *Dictionary*, pp. XXXI and 1272).

2) While the preface of *document Pelliot* (V. 13) has *ạdsin-la*. In V. 3 *rkyen*, while *rkyond* is repeatedly found in the fragments of *Çālistambasūtra*; in V. 14 *ston ni* instead of *stond ni*; in V. 23 *rton cig* instead of *rtond cig*. But in the latter example, *cig* in the place of *žig*, as required by the present rule, is testimony of the effect of a *da drag*; the palatal *c* or *č* is certainly a composite sound of the value of *tš*, and, though not actually written, the *da drag* may have nevertheless been actually sounded — *rtont-tšig*.

as purely euphonic (*brjod bde-ba*), and there is surely much in favor of such a view, at least in the final stage of the development of the matter, though this does not exclude the idea that in a former period of the language a more specific function of a formative character may have been attached to it. When in the fragments of the *Çālistambasūtra* the adverb *on kyaṅ* is written *ond kyaṅ*, we doubtless have here a wholly secondary application suggested by analogy where no other than a euphonic reason for the presence of *d* can be given; for the element *on* has arisen from *o-na* ("if this is so"), hence the *d* cannot have originally inhered in it, but must be a later addition to facilitate pronunciation (comparable to the French euphonic *t* in *a-t-il*, etc.). The euphonic character of *da drag* is visible also in its restriction to stems terminating in *n*, *r*, *l*; and even in these limited groups a certain selection seems to take place, in that certain stems are not capable of receiving it, as evidenced by the examples quoted, and many others occurring in literature. Thus, *t'ar-ba* forms only *t'ar-ro*, never *t'ar-to*, while *skul-ba* always forms *bskul-to*. An interesting case is presented by the verb *skur-ba*, which in the sense "to abuse" forms *skur-ro*, but in the sense "to send" *skur-to*. Here we almost gain the impression that the additional *d* was resorted to in order to discriminate between two different homophonous words.

In questioning the formative elements of the language, we observe that there is an affix *-d* forming transitive verbs from intransitive or nominal roots: for example, *skye-ba*, "to be born," — *skye-d-pa*, "to beget;" *nu-ma*, "breast," — *nu-d-pa*, "to suckle;" *ḥbye-ba*, "to open" (intr.), *ḥbye-d-pa*, "to open" (tr.); *ḥdu-ba*, "to assemble" (intr.) — *sdu-d-pa*, "to assemble, gather" (tr.); *ḥbu-ba*, "to be lighted, 'kindled," — *ḥbu-d-pa*, "to blow;" *dma*, "low," — *smo-d* (*dmo-d*)-*pa*, "to blame, contempt." [1]) Also *byed-pa*, "to do," compared with *bya*, "to be done, action," belongs here; and I am inclined to think that *byed* (phonetically *byöd* or *b'öd*) has arisen from a contraction of *bya* + *yod*, *lit.* "he is doing." It is conceivable that this final *-d* may in general be a remnant of the copula *yod*: as, for instance, *sgo ḁbye*, "the door is open;" *sgo ḁbyed* (= *ḁbye* + *yod*, *ḁbyöd*), "(I am) opening the door." This possible origin of the transitive *-d* would account also for the fact that formations with *-d* denote a state or condition, as there are *rga-d-pa*, "old man," from *rga-ba*, "to be old;" *na-d*, "disease," from *na-ba*, "to be sick." If this *-d* is a survival of a former *yod*, then *nad* formed of *na* + *yod* is "the state of being ill;" *rgad* formed of *rga* + *yod* is literally "one being old." Likewise we have *ḁgro-ba* and *ḁgrod-pa* (also *bgrod-pa*), "to go, travel," without apparent distinction of meaning at present, while the latter originally meant "to be on a journey."

The conclusions to be derived from these considerations may be summed up as follows. It is probable that the so-called *da drag*, in the beginning, was a formative element of grammatical character, or at least derived from such an element. In the earliest period of literature, this significance had entirely vanished from the consciousness of the speakers; and we then find the *d* applied in the *n*, *r*, and *l* stems inserted between stem and suffix for purely euphonic reasons. The degree to which the euphonic *d* was culti-

---

1) Compare SHTSHERBATSKOI in *Collection of Articles in Honor of Lamanski* (Vol. I, p. 646, St. Petersburg, 1907). The author who abstains from indicating what he owes to his predecessors is neither the discoverer of this law nor others propounded by him. The case under consideration has already been treated by A. CONRADY (*Eine indochinesische Causativ-Denominativ-Bildung*, p. 45); before the time when Professor Conrady published his fundamental book, I enjoyed the privilege, in the course of over a year, of being engaged with him in so many discussions of the Tibetan verb, that I am no longer conscious of what is originally due to him or to me.

vated must have varied in different localities, or, what amounts to the same, dialects; it was not a stable or an indispensable constituent of the language, but could be used with a certain amount of freedom. This accounts for its uncertainty in writing, being omitted in some ancient documents, and being fixed in others, and even in these not consistently. The state of writing, in this case, does not allow of any safe inferences as to phonetic facts. In the spellings *t-o*, *t-am*, *t-u*, still in vogue in the modern written language, the *da drag* is practically preserved, the alteration inspired by simplification being of a graphic, not phonetic nature. For this reason it is justifiable to conclude that also in other cases the *da drag*, without its specification in writing, may have continued to be articulated.

## Phonology of the Tibetan Language of the Ninth Century.

The Tibetan scholars distinguish two main periods in the development of their language, which they designate as "old language" (*brda rñiṅ*) and "new language" (*brda gsar*).[1] The difference between the two is largely lexicographical and phonetical, the latter distinction being reflected in the mode of spelling; the grammatical differences are but slight, while stylistic variation commands a wide latitude. The existence of a large number of archaic terms in the older writings, no longer understood at present, has led the Tibetans to prepare extensive glossaries, in which those words and

1) The translations "old and new orthography" proposed by JÄSCHKE (*Dictionary*, p. 298) take the meaning of these terms in too narrow a sense. Questions of spelling in Tibetan are at the same time those of phonetics and grammar, and in the native glossaries the two terms strictly refer to old and new words. They consequently bear on grammar and lexicography, and comprise the language in its total range. For the distinctions made by Mr. WADDELL (*J. R. A. S.*, 1909, pp. 1269, 1275) of pre-classic and classic periods (even "fully-fledged classical style," and semi-classic, p. 945) I see no necessity; the Tibetan division is clear and to the point, and is quite sufficient.

phrases are defined in modern language. The most useful of these works is the *Li-šii gur k'aṅ.*[1] The well-known dictionary *rTogs-par sla-ba*[2] contains a long list of such words in verses; and the lCaṅ-skya Hutuktu of Peking, Rol-pai rdo-rje (Lalitavajra), a voluminous writer, who has composed a number of special glossaries for various departments of literature, offers in this series a "List of ancient compared with the modern words" (*brda gsar rñiṅ-gi skor*).[3] There is, further, a work under the title *Bod yul-gyi skad gsar rñiṅ-gi rnam-par dbye-ba rta bdun snaṅ-ba,* which has been carefully utilized in the "Dictionnaire thibétain-latin-français par les Missionnaires catholiques du Thibet" (Hongkong, 1899).[4] It is a particular merit of this dictionary that the words and phrases of the ancient style are clearly indicated as such, and identified with the corresponding terms of the modern style (by the reference *A = R, ancien = récent*). This as well as another feature, the treatment of synonyms, constitutes a point in which the French work is superior to Jäschke. Jäschke, it is true, includes a goodly number of archaisms (though far from being complete), but in most cases does not indicate them as such. As regards spelling, the

---

1) Schmidt and Boehtlingk's *Verzeichnis,* p. 64; Schiefner, *Mélanges asiatiques,* Vol. I, p. 3. There is a good Peking edition (26 fols.) with interlinear Mongol version, printed in 1741.

2) *Keleti szemle,* 1907, p. 181.

3) It is published in Vol. 7 of his Collected Works (*gsuṅ ḥbum*) printed in Peking (compare *Mélanges asiatiques,* Vol. I, p. 411).

4) According to kind information given by Father A. Desgodins in a letter dated from Hongkong, October 7, 1901. Father Desgodins, with whom I was in correspondence on Tibetan subjects from 1897 to 1901, and whose memory is very dear to me, was good enough to furnish me with a list of the seven Tibetan dictionaries compiled for his great enterprise. It was at my instigation that Father Desgodins consented to send to Europe the single sheets of his Dictionary as they left the press, so that I was in a position to make practical use of his material in my work as early as 1897 and 1898. It seems singular that, perhaps with the sole exception of Mr. v. Zach, I have thus far remained alone in recognizing the special importance of this dictionary and the way of using it.

system now generally adopted is traced by Tibetan tradition to the reform of two scholars, dPal-brtsegs (Çrīkūṭa) from sKa-ba, [1]) and kLui rgyal-mtsʿan (Nāgadhvaja) from Cog-ro, [2]) assisted by a staff of scholars, at the time of King Kʿri-lde sroṅ-btsan (first part of the ninth century; according to *Tʿang shu*, his reign began in 816).[3]) Prior to this time, as we are informed by Rin-cʿen cʿos skyoṅ bzaṅ-po (1440—1526) in his remarkable work *Za-ma-tog*, there were different systems of spelling in vogue, but all traceable

---

1) dPal-brtsegs took part in the redaction of the first catalogue of the Tibetan Tripiṭaka (*Dokumente*, I, pp. 50—51), was familiar with the Chinese language (*Roman*, p. 4), and figures as translator in the Kanjur (*Annales du Musée Guimet*, Vol. II, pp. 182, 233, 337). In the Tanjur, for instance, he cooperated with Sarvajñadeva in the translation of Nāgārjuna's Suhṛillekha (translated by H. Wenzel, p. 32), and in that of Candragomin's Çikshalekha (ed. by A. Ivanovski, *Zap.*, Vol. IV, pp. 53—81). His portrait is in Grünwedel, *Mythologie des Buddhismus*, p. 49.

2) This name occurs in the list of names of the Tibetan ministers in the Lhasa inscription of 822 reproduced by Bushell (*The Early History of Tibet*, *J. R. A. S.*, 1880); he belonged to the Board of Ministers of Foreign Affairs (*pʿyi blon bka-la gtogs-pa*). The name *Cog* (or *Čog*) *-ro* is transcribed in Chinese *Shu-lu* 屬盧, which indicates that the former character was sounded in the Tʿang period *čuk* (compare Hakka *chuk*, Yang-chou *tsuk*, Hokk. *čiuk*, and Conrady, *Eine indochinesische Causativ-Denominativ-Bildung*, p. 165). An analogous case occurs in *Yüan shi*: 搠思 = Tib. *cʿos*, indicated by Pelliot (*Journal asiatique*, Mars-Avril, 1913, p. 456), and formerly by E. v. Zach (*China Review*, Vol. XXIV, 1900, p. 256b). Compare p. 75, No. 14.

3) This king was honored with the epithet *Ral-pa-can* (Skr. *kesarin*), "wearing long hair," because he wore his hair in long flowing locks. F. Köppen (*Die lamaische Hierarchie und Kirche*, p. 72), with his sarcastic humor, has described how the weak and bigot monarch became a plaything in the hands of the clergy and allowed the Lamas to sit on the ribbons fastened to his locks; he intended, of course, to imbibe the strength and holiness of the clergy. Mr. Waddell (*J. R. A. S.*, 1909, p. 1253) tries to establish two new facts, — first that the king wore a cue, and secondly that the cue is a Chinese custom introduced by the king into Tibet (the undignified vernacular word "pigtail" used by Mr. Waddell, in my opinion, is out of place in an historical treatise). The attribution of a cue to the king is a rather inconsiderate invention. No Tibetan tradition ascribes to him a cue or its introduction from China; on the contrary, it is expressly related that the ribbons mentioned above were fastened to the hair of his head (*dbu skra*, see *dPag bsam ljon bzaṅ*, p. 175, line 14). The difference between wearing long hair and a cue is self-evident. Neither could the king have introduced any cue from China, since in the age of the Tʿang dynasty, as known to every one, the Chinese did not wear cues; nor is the cue a Chinese invention at all.

to the teachings of T$^{c}$on-mi Saṁbhoṭa, who, during the reign of King Sroṅ-btsan sgam-po (seventh century), introduced writing from India to Tibet.[1]) That reform of the language is expressly recorded in Tibetan history. I. J. SCHMIDT[2]) has already pointed out this fact from the *Bodhi-mōr*, the Kalmuk version of the Tibetan *rGyal rabs*, where it is said that at the time of King K$^{c}$ri-lde sroṅ-btsan (the name as given by SCHMIDT is erroneous), besides the new translations, also all previous translations were "recast and rendered clearer according to a more recent and corrected language." In *dPag bsam ljon bzaṅ* (p. 175, line 12) the same is told still more distinctly in the words that the translations were made afresh (*gsar-du aṅ*) in a newly cast language. The reflex of this tradition is conspicuous in the colophons of numerous treatises of the Kanjur translated at that period, where we meet the same phrase, *skad gsar c$^{c}$ad kyis kyaṅ bcos-nas gtan-la p$^{c}$ab-pa.*

In order to study successfully the phonology of a Tibetan text of the ninth century, it is an essential point to form a correct idea of the condition of the language in that period. This task has not yet been attempted. The material for the solution of this

1) It is known to what fanciful conclusions Messrs. BARNETT (*J. R. A. S.*, 1903, p. 112) and FRANCKE (*Ancient Khotan*, p. 565; *Indian Antiquary*, 1903, p. 363; *Mem. A. S. B.*, Vol. I, 1905, p. 44) have been driven in regard to the introduction of Tibetan writing. Mr. BARNETT, sensibly enough, later withdrew his former view; while Mr. FRANCKE, who stamps as a myth, without any historical criticism, every Tibetan account not suiting his fancy, continues to create his own mythology. There is no reason to dwell on these fantasies, or to waste time in their discussion. Mr. WADDELL (*J. R. A. S.*, 1909, pp. 945—947) has already risen against these views with what seems to me to be perfect justice, and it gives me pleasure to acknowledge that I fully concur in Mr. WADDELL's opinion on this point.

2) *Geschichte der Ost-Mongolen*, p. 358. The passage of *rGyal rabs* (fol. 80) runs thus: *c'os t'ams-cad skad gsar bcad-kyis gtan-la p'ab*, "all religious treatises were cast into a new language and re-edited." JÄSCHKE translates the phrase *gsar gcod-pa* by "to inquire into, investigate, examine;" but the literal significance is "to cut anew, to do something from a fresh start, to recast." An examination of the language of the texts would have sense only if alterations in the language, its style, phonology, and spelling, were to be made.

problem is deposited in the Tibeto-Chinese inscriptions of the T'ang period and in the Chinese transcriptions of Tibetan words embodied in the Chinese Annals of the T'ang Dynasty. The bilingual epigraphical material in which Tibetan words are recorded, in comparison with their renderings in Chinese characters reproducing the contemporaneous Tibetan pronunciation of the language of Lhasa, is of primary importance; for it enables us to frame certain conclusions as to the Chinese method of transcribing Tibetan sounds, and to restore the Tibetan pronunciation of the ninth century on the basis of the ancient Chinese sounds. Thus equipped with a certain fund of laws, we may hope to attack the Tibetan words in the T'ang Annals. The most important document for our purpose is the sworn treaty concluded between Tibet and China in 821, and commemorated on stone in 822, known to the Chinese archæologists under the name *T'ang T'u-po hui mêng pei* 唐吐蕃會盟碑. This inscription has been made the object of a remarkable study by the eminent scholar Lo Chên-yü 羅振玉 in No. 7 of the journal *Shên chou kuo kuang tsi* (Shanghai, 1909).[1]) This article is accompanied by two half-tone plates reproducing the four sides of the stone monument erected in Lhasa, which is 14 feet 7 inches (Chinese) high and 3 feet 1½ inches wide. The recto contains a parallel Tibetan and Chinese text; the verso, a Tibetan text exclusively. The lateral surfaces are covered with the names of the ministers who swore to the treaty. There were seventeen Tibetan and seventeen Chinese officials participating in the ratification. The names of the Tibetan officials are grouped on one of the small sides; those of the Chinese, on the other. Both series of names are given in interlinear versions, — the Tibetan names being transcribed in Chinese, the Chinese names in Tibetan. It is obvious that from

1) Compare P. PELLIOT, *B. E. F. E. O.*, Vol. IX, 1909, p. 578.

a philological point of view, material of the first order is here offered to us. From the reproductions of Lo Chên-yü it follows that BUSHELL, [1]) who has given a translation of the Chinese text, [2]) merely reproduced half of the stone. The first plate attached to his paper contains the list of the Tibetan ministers, which is, accordingly, one of the small sides of the stone; this part is not translated by Bushell or referred to in his text; his second plate gives the recto of the stone, while the verso and the other small side with the names of the Chinese ministers are wanting. Bushell's photo-lithographic reproduction is very readable, and my reading of the Tibetan names is based on his Plate I. The Chinese reproduction is too much reduced, and the glossy paper on which it is printed considerably enhances the difficulty of reading. But Lo Chên-yü deserves our thanks for having added in print a transcript of the entire Chinese portion of the monument, inclusive of the thirty-four names as far as decipherable; this part of his work proved to me of great utility, as Bushell's small scale reproduction, in many

1) *The Early History of Tibet* (*J. R. A. S.*, 1880).

2) A drawback to BUSHELL's translation is that it appears as a solid coherent account, without indication of the many gaps in the text. Bushell filled these from the text as published in the *Ta Ts'ing i t'ung chi*. As the notes of Lo Chên-yü rectify and supplement this edition of the text on several points, a new translation of this important monument would not be a futile task, if made on the basis of Lo Chên-yü's transcript, in which the lacunes are exactly indicated. — A. H. FRANCKE (*Epigraphia Indica*, Vol. X, 1909—10, pp. 89—93) has given, after BUSHELL's rubbing (Pl. II), a transcript of the Tibetan version, and what, from a Tibetan point of view, he believes to be a translation of it. BUSHELL's Plate I, the list of the Tibetan officials, is not mentioned by Francke. It goes without saying that this Tibetan text, as well as the other Tibetan epigraphical documents of the T'ang period, cannot be translated merely by the aid of our imperfect Tibetan dictionaries; sinology is somewhat needed to do them. These documents were drafted in the Tibeto-Chinese government chancery of Lhasa; and the Tibetan phraseology is to some extent modelled after the Chinese documentary style, and must be carefully studied in the light of the latter. BUSHELL (p. 102), it seems to me, is not correct in stating that the Chinese text of the monument is a translation of the Tibetan original; the question as to which of the two is the original is immaterial. Both express the same sense, and were drafted simultaneously by the Tibeto-Chinese clerical staff of Lhasa.

passages, left me in the lurch. The account of the erection of the monument as given in the Tibetan annals (*rGyal rabs*, fol. 92) may be of some interest. "During the reign of King Ral-pa-can, the son-in-law and father-in-law [the sovereigns of Tibet and China] were still in a state of war, and the Tibetan army, several tens of thousands, conquered all fortified places of China. The Ho-shang of China and the clergy of Tibet intervened and concluded a sworn pact. The son-in-law despatched pleasing gifts, and an honest agreement was reached. In the frontier-post rMe-ru in China, the two sovereigns each erected a temple and had a design of sun and moon engraved on a bowlder, which was to symbolize that, as sun and moon form a pair in the sky, so the sovereign son-in-law and father-in-law are on earth. It was agreed that the Tibetan army should not advance below rMe-ru in China, or the Chinese army above this place. In order to preserve the boundary-line, they erected visible landmarks in the shape of earth-mounds where earth was available, or stone-heaps where stone was available. Then they fixed regulations vouching for the prosperity of Tibet and China, and invoking as witnesses the Triratna, Sun and Moon, Stars and Planets, and the gods of vengeance,[1])

---

1) This passage occurs in the inscription 三寳及諸賢聖日月星辰請爲知 (BUSHELL: 和) 證. Tib. (line 62) *dkon mc'og gsum dan ap'ags-pai dam-pa-rnams gñi zla dan gza skar-la yan dpan-du gsol-te*, "the Three Precious Ones (Skr. *triratna*), the Venerable Saints, Sun and Moon, Planets and Stars they invoked as witnesses." Mr. FRANCKE (*l. c.*, p. 98) translates, "The three gods(!), the august heaven, etc., are asked to witness it." He has the wrong reading *ap'ags-pai nam-k'a* where *dam-pa*, "holy," is clearly in the text; the plural suffix *rnams* is inferred by me from the context (the stone is mutilated in this spot). The Tibetan phrase, as read by me, exactly corresponds in meaning to the Chinese *chu hien shêng*, "the holy sages." There is no word for "heaven" in the Chinese text, nor a Tibetan word for "heaven" in the above corresponding passage in *rGyal rabs*; consequently *nam-k'a* cannot be sought in the Tibetan version of the inscription, either. The gods of vengeance (*lha gñan rnams*) are omitted in the inscription, presumably for the reason that no exact Chinese equivalent for this Tibetan term could be found. The interpretation as above given is derived from JÄSCHKE (*Dictionary*, p. 192), with whom I. J. SCHMIDT (*Geschichte der Ost-Mongolen*, p. 361), translating from the *Bodhi-mör* ("die rächenden Tenggeri"), agrees. The *gñan* are a class

the two sovereigns swore a solemn oath by their heads.[1]) The text of

---

of demons whose specific nature is still somewhat uncertain; in the Bon religion they form a triad with the *klu* and *sa bdag* (see the writer's *Ein Sühngedicht der Bonpo*). The word *gñan* means also a species of wild sheep, argali (*Ovis ammon* L. or *Ovis Hodgsoni* Blyth., see M. DAUVERGNE, *Bull. Musée d'hist. nat.*, Vol. IV, 1898, p. 216; the definition of CHANDRA DAS [*Dictionary*, p. 490] — "not the *Ovis ammon* but the *Ovis Hodgsoni*" — is wrong, as both names, in fact, refer to the same species). Now, we read in *Kiu T'ang shu* (Ch. 196 上, p. 1b), in regard to the ancient T'u-po, 事羱羝之神, "they serve the spirits of *nguan ti*;" *nguan* (this reading is given in the Glossary of *T'ang shu*, Ch. 23, by the characters 吾官 *ngu kuan*; Tib. *gñan* and Chin. *ṅuan* are perhaps allied words; *Erh ya* reads *yüan* 元) likewise refers to a species of wild sheep or argali, and *ti* is a ram. We know nothing to the effect that the Tibetans ever worshipped argali, nor can the Chinese words be explained as the transcription of a Tibetan word. It seems to me that Chin. *nguan ti* is a literal translation of a Tib. *gñan-p'o* (or *-p'a*, "male of an animal") caused by the double significance of the Tibetan word *gñan*, and that the Chinese annalist means to convey the idea that the Tibetans worship a class of spirits styled *gñan*. On two former occasions it was pointed out by me that the word *gñan*, presumably for euphemistic reasons, is frequently written *gñen* ("friend, helper"). In the Table of *document Pelliot* (V, 3) we meet the oracle, *gñen lha skyes-po-la ạts'o-ba-žig oṅ-bar ston*, where I am under the impression that *gñen lha* should be taken in the sense of *gñan lha*, and accordingly be translated, "It indicates that a terrific spirit doing harm to men will come" (the injury is not done to the god, as M. BACOT translates).

1) Tib. *dbu bsñuṅ daṅ bro bor-ro.* JÄSCHKE (*Dictionary*, p. 382a) has already given the correct translation of this phrase. Mr. WADDELL (*J. R. A. S.*, 1909, p. 1270) has misunderstood it by translating *dbu sñuṅ gnaṅ-ste* "(the king) was sick with his head." The word *sñuṅ* in this passage has nothing to do with the word *sñuṅ*, "disease," but is the verb *sñuṅ-ba* (causative from *ṅuṅ-ba*, "small"), "to make small, diminish, reduce." The phrase *dbu sñuṅ* is a form of adjuration corresponding to our "I will lose my head, if..." The beginning of the inscription therefore is, "Land was granted (*sa gnaṅ*, which does not mean 'honor be given')... The father, the sovereign K'ri-sroṅ lde-btsan [the translation "the king's father's father" is wrong; the father, *yab*, is a well-known attribute of King K'ri-sroṅ] formerly made the grant under his oath." On this mistranslation the following speculation is based (p. 1268): "King K'ri-sroṅ lde-btsan is stigmatized as being of unsound mind — a condition regarding which there never has been the slightest hint in the national histories — and the rule of the kings generally is declared to have caused a cycle of misfortunes to the country." The entire "historical" interpretation of this inscription is unfortunately not based on the national histories, but is a dream of the author. There is nothing in the text of "the Sacred Cross of the Bon," which is plainly a Svastika designed on the silver patent (*dṅul-gyi yi-ge*, translation of *yin p'ai* 銀牌), nor is there "the P'an country of the Secret Presence of the Bon deity," which simply means "the district of *ạP'an* in *sKu sruṅs*" (name of a locality). Neither the translation nor the explanation of this inscription can be accepted.

the treaty was inscribed on three stone tablets. On the two large surfaces was written the text containing the sworn treaty concluded between the two sovereigns; on the two small sides of the stone was written the list of the names [1]) of the Tibetan and Chinese officials who were accredited as ministers of state. One of these stone monuments was erected at Lhasa, another in front of the palace of the Chinese emperor, another at rMe-ru on the frontier of China and Tibet. 'If regardless of the text of this treaty, the Tibetans should march their army into China, the Chinese should read three times the text of the inscription in front of the palace of the emperor of China, — then the Tibetans will all be vanquished. On the other hand, if the Chinese should march their army into Tibet, all Chinese will be vanquished in case the text of the inscription of Lhasa should three times be read,' — this oath was stipulated between the state ministers of Tibet and China and sealed with the signets of the two sovereigns."

The purpose of the following study is purely philological, not epigraphical or historical, though it simultaneously furnishes a not unimportant contribution to the then existing offices in Tibet; the latter subject, however, calls for a special investigation, for which also the numerous references in the Tibetan annals must be utilized, and it is therefore here discarded for the time being. The inquiry is restricted to the Chinese transcriptions of Tibetan words; their pronunciation is ascertained by restoring, as far as possible, the Chinese sounds, such as were in vogue during the T'ang period. It will be recognized that the Chinese applied a rigorous and logical method to their transcriptions of Tibetan words, and that in this manner a solid basis is obtained for framing a number of

1) Tib. *miṅ rus*. The same expression written *myiṅ rus* occurs likewise in the inscription of 822 (compare No. 12, p. 74), where it corresponds to Chin. *ming wei* 名位.

important conclusions as to the state of Tibetan phonology in the ninth century, with entirely convincing results, which are fully confirmed by the conditions of the ancient Tibetan documents. First the material itself is reviewed, to place everybody in a position to form his own opinion, then the conclusions to be drawn from it are discussed. The single items are numbered in the same manner as has been done by Lo Chên-yü. Nos. 1—3 contain no transcriptions, and are therefore of no avail for our purpose; in Nos. 4—8, the Tibetan text, with the exception of a few words, is hopelessly destroyed. Nos. 9—20 run as follows:

9. *Cʿab-srid-kyi̥* [1]) *blon-po cʿen-po žaṅ kʿri̥ btsan* [2]) *kʿod ne staṅ* = 宰相同平章事尚綺立贊窟寧思當 *tsʿai siang tʿung pʿing chang shi shang kʿi li tsan kʿu(t) ning se tang*. The name of this minister, accordingly, was sounded *kʿri tsan kʿod(t) ne̥* [3]) *staṅ*. His Tibetan title means "great minister of state," rendered into Chinese "minister and superintendent of affairs." [4])

10. *Cʿab-srid-kyi̥ blon-po cʿen-po žaṅ kʿri̥ bžer lta mtʿoṅ* = 宰相同平章事尚綺立熱 [5]) 貪通 *tsʿai siang tʿung pʿing chang shi shang kʿi li že (je) tʿam (tʿan) tʿung*. The Tibetan name of this minister, accordingly, was articulated *kʿri že(r) tam-tʿoṅ* (for explanation see farther on).

1) By the transcription *i̥* the inverted vowel sign *i* commented on p. 53 should be understood. Its phonetic value will be discussed hereafter.

2) The two words *kʿri̥ btsan* are destroyed on the stone, but can be correctly restored on the basis of the Chinese equivalents *kʿi li tsan*; Chin. *kʿi li* corresponds to Tib. *kʿri̥* in No. 10, and Chin. *tsan* is the frequent and regular transcription of Tib. *btsan*.

3) As indicated by Chin. *ning*, the vowel of Tib. *ne* was nasalized (pronounced like French *nain*).

4) See GILES, *Dictionary*, 2d ed., p. 1132b.

5) Lo Chên-yü transcribes this character 慹, but this is an error. The reproduction of BUSHELL shows that the character is as given above, and this is the one required for the rendering of the Tibetan sounds. This reading, moreover, is confirmed by *Kiu Tʿang shu* (Ch. 196 下, p. 11b), where exactly the same personage is mentioned 尚綺立熱 who in 825 was sent on a friendly mission to the Chinese Court.

11. *C$^{c}$ab-srid-kyi̥ blon-po c$^{c}$en-po blon rgyal bzaṅ ạdus kuṅ* [1]) = 宰相同平章事論頰藏弩思恭 *ts$^{c}$ai siang t$^{c}$ung p$^{c}$ing chang shi lun kia(p)* (*γ'ap*) *tsang* [2]) *nu* [3]) *se kuṅ*. The name of this minister was pronounced *g'al* (or *γ'al*) *zaṅ dus kuṅ*.

12. *Bod c$^{c}$en-poi̥ blon-po ts$^{c}$al-gyi t$^{c}$abs daṅ myiṅ̥ rus* = 大蕃諸寮案登壇者名位 *Ta Po chu liao ngan têng t$^{c}$an che ming wei*. The Tibetan is a free translation from Chinese, the phrase *têng t$^{c}$an*, "those who ascended the altar" (in order to swear to the treaty) being omitted. Note that *Bod c$^{c}$en-po*, "Great *Bod*," does not occur in Tibetan records, but is only a stock phrase modelled in the Tibeto-Chinese chancery of Lhasa after the Great T$^{c}$ang Dynasty 大唐.

13. *naṅ blon mc$^{c}$ims žaṅ rgyal bžer k$^{c}$on ne btsan* = 曩論琛尙頰熱窟寧贊 *nang lun ch$^{c}$êm* (*ch$^{c}$ên*) *shang kia(p)* (*γ'ap*) *že* (*je*) *k$^{c}$u(t) ning tsan*. In the name of the Minister of the Interior we note the pronunciations *c$^{c}$im* (or *č$^{c}$im*) for *mc$^{c}$ims*, *že* for *bžer*, and again the nasalized vowel in *nẹ*.

14. *p$^{c}$yi̥ blon bka-la gtogs-pa Cog-ro* | *blon btsan bžer lto goṅ* =

1) In Bushell's reproduction, *kaṅ*. But the rubbing was sharply cut off around these last two words, so that the sign *u* may have been lost during this process. The Chinese transcription *kung* calls for a Tibetan *kong* or *kung*.

2) It doubtless represents an ancient **zang* (**dzang*); compare the Japanese reading *zō*. Also in *Yüan shi* Tib. *bzaṅ-po* is transcribed 藏卜 and Tib. *blo bzaṅ* 羅藏 (E. v. ZACH, *Tibetica*, *China Review*, Vol. XXIV, 1900, p. 256a). The character 臧 *tsang* serves in *T'ang shu* (Ch. 216 下, p. 6a) to render Tib. *gtsaṅ*, the name of the main river of Central Tibet.

3) *Nu* 弩 seems to have had the phonetic value *du* (Japanese *do*), and *du se* is intended for Tib. *ạdus*. An analogous example occurs in *Kiu T'ang shu* in the name of the Tibetan king *K'i nu si lung* 器弩悉弄 answering to Tib. *K'ri du sroṅ* (usually styled *Du sroṅ maṅ-po*). Compare *lo* 羅 transcribing Turkish *dü* (CHAVANNES and PELLIOT, *Journal asiatique*, 1913, No. 1, p. 175). The character *lie* 獵 rendering Tib. *lde* (pronounced *de* in the ninth century) in the name of King *K'ri sroṅ lde btsan* 乞黎蘇籠 | 贊 (*Kiu T'ang shu*, Ch. 196 上, p. 8b), offers another instance of Chinese initial *l* corresponding to *d* in a foreign language.

紕論伽羅篤波屬盧論贊熱土公 *pʻi lun kia lo*[1]) *tu*(*k*) *po šu* (*čuk*) *lu lun tsan že* (*je*) *tʻu kung*. The Tibetan words were accordingly articulated at that time, *pʻʻi lon ka-la tog-pa* (the Minister of Foreign Affairs) *čog-ro lon tsan že*(*r*) *to goṅ*.

15. *snam pʻyi-pa mcʻims žaṅ brtan bžer snag*[2]) *cig* = 思南紕波琛尙且熱思諾市 *se nam* (*nan*) *pʻi po chʻêm* (*chʻên*) *shang tan že* (*je*) *se nak* (*no*) *shi*. Tibetan pronunciation, *snam pʻʻi-pa cʻim žaṅ tan že*(*r*) *snag*(*k*) *ci°*.

16. *mṅan pon baṅ-so o-cog gi blo ąbal blon kru bzaṅ gyes rma* = 岸奔猛蘇戶屬勃羅末論矩立藏〇摩[3]) *ngan pên* (*pön*, *pun*) *mong* (Cantonese and Hakka *mang*, Japanese *bō*) *su hu* (Cantonese *u*, Ningpo *wu*, Japanese *o*)[4]) *šu* (**čuk*) *pu lo mo* (Hakka

---

1) Sounded *la*; see VOLPICELLI, *Prononciation ancienne du chinois*, pp. 161, 181, 183 (*Actes XIe Congrès Or.*, Paris, 1898).

2) Written as if it were *stag*, but the seeming *t* may have been intended for *n* which is required by the Chinese transcript; likewise in No. 17. The palaeographic features of Tibetan epigraphy of the Tʻang period remain to be studied in detail. — The character 諾 is sounded *nak* in Korean, *naku* in Japanese. The phonetic element 若 has the value *nik*; in the Manichean treatise translated by M. CHAVANNES and M. PELLIOT (*Journal asiatique*, 1911, No. 8, p. 538) it is combined with the radical 口 into a character which otherwise does not occur; but as the Pahlavī equivalent rendered by it is *nag*, this artificial character must have had also the sound *nak*, in the same manner as 諾.

3) Lo Chên-yü transcribes the last two characters 名〇. The first of these does not seem to be 名, though I cannot make it out in the reproduction of BUSHELL, which is too much reduced; but 名 cannot be the correct reading, as the sound *ming* is incapable of reproducing anything like Tib. *gyes*. The second character left a blank by Lo, I distinctly read *mo* (anciently *ma*), as above, in BUSHELL's plate, and this very well answers as transcription of Tib. *rma* (sounded *ma*).

4) The equation 戶 = Tib. *o* allows us to restore theoretically the name (姓) of King *Kʻri sroṅ lde btsan* given in *Tʻang shu* (Ch. 216 下, p. 1b) in the form *Hu lu tʻi* 戶盧提 into Tib. *O ro lde*. Chin. *lu* = Tib. *ro* we had in No. 14. The ancient sounds of *tʻi* were **te, de* (Japanese *tei, dei*), hence Tib. *de* or *lde* frequently occurring in the names of the kings may be inferred (it occurs likewise in the name of the ancestor 祖 of the Tibetans, *Hu tʻi pu si ye* 鶻提勃悉野 where *tʻi pu* corresponds to Tib. *de-po* or *lde-po*; the other elements of this name are treated farther on). A name of the form *O ro lde*, however, does not occur in Tibetan records; but in

*mat*, Korean *mal*; ancient sounds **mwat* and *mwar*[1])) *lun kü li tsang* ○ *mo* (*ma*). The sign of the genitive, *gi*, is not transcribed in Chinese. Tib. *mṅan*, accordingly, was sounded *ṅan*; *blo* was sounded *blo* (Chin. *pu-lo*), not *lo*, as at present; *ạbal* was sounded *bal*, or possibly *mbal* or *mwal*; *kru* was sounded *kru* (Chin. *kü-li*), not as now *tru* or *ṭu*; *rma* was sounded *ma*. Tib. *mṅan pon* must be a compound written for *mṅa dpon* ("rulers and lords"), the prefix *d* being altered into *n* under the influence of the initial guttural nasal *ṅ* and then pronounced and written *ṅan pon*. The meaning of the above passage is, "The minister *Kru bzaṅ gyes rma*, who was in charge of the sepulchres of the sovereigns and lords." It was hitherto unknown that such an office existed in Tibet, and this fact is of great culture-historical interest. We know that the ancient kings of Tibet were buried under elevated tumuli, and the *rGyal rabs* has carefully recorded the exact locality and its name where each king was interred.[2]) The *T'ang shu* (Ch. 216 下, p. 6) imparts a

the inscription of 783 edited and translated by Mr. WADDELL (*J. R. A. S.*, 1909, p. 931) the name of a primeval king *O lde spu rgyal* is mentioned. I am therefore inclined to regard the Chinese transcription *Hu lu t'i* as a reproduction of Tib. *O lde*, the Chinese syllable *lu* rendering the prefix *l* in *lde*, which was sounded on account of the preceding vowel, as still at present the prefix is articulated in the second element of a compound when the first terminates in a vowel. The name *O lde* has not yet been pointed out as a name or title of King *K'ri-sroṅ* in any Tibetan document; it remains to be seen whether it will be confirmed. The comment made by Mr. WADDELL (p. 983) on the king named *O lde spu rgyal* is erroneous; he does not follow the Seven Celestial Rulers in Tibetan tradition. This king whom Mr. WADDELL has in mind is styled in *rGyal rabs* "*Spu de guṅ rgyal*" (mentioned also by ROCKHILL, *The Life of the Buddha*, p. 209, but the name does not mean "the tiger-haired king"), but there is no reason to assume that he is identical with *O lde spu rgyal*. Although Mr. WADDELL (p. 949, note 3) expressly states that there seemed no trace of a final *d* in the word *o*, Mr. A. H. FRANCKE (*J. A. S. B.*, Vol. VI, 1910, p. 94) boldly and arbitrarily alters this name into *Od lde spu rgyal*, and translates this *Od lde* by "beautiful light," which is pure fancy, as is the whole article in which Mr. FRANCKE, to his great satisfaction, shifts the theatre of action of Tibetan tradition connected with King *gÑa k'ri btsan-po* from central to western Tibet.

1) CHAVANNES and PELLIOT, *Journal asiatique*, 1911, No. 3, p. 519.

2) The interment of King Sroṅ-btsan sgam-po is thus described in *rGyal rabs* (Ch.

vivid description of the sepulchral mounds 丘墓 of the Tibetan nobles scattered along the upper course of the Huang-ho, white tigers being painted on the red-plastered walls of the buildings belonging to the tombs; when alive, they donned a tigers-kin in battle, so the tiger was the emblem of their valor after death.

17. *bkai p<sup></sup>*

17. *bkaị pʻrin blon cʻen* 1) *ka* 2) *blon snag bžer ha ñen* = 給事中勃○伽論思諾熱合軋 *ki shi chung pʻo* (*pu*) ○ *kia lun se nak* (*no*) *že* (*je*) *ha* (*ho*) *yen.*

18. *rtsis-pa cʻen-po* ○ 3) *blon stag zịgs rgan kʻod* = 資思波折逋額論思○4)昔幹窟 *tse-se po chʻê pu ngo*(*k*) *lun*

---

18, fol. 76): "His sepulchre (*bañ-so*) was erected at ạCʻoñ-po (in Yar-luñ), being a mile all around. It was quadrangular in shape, and there was a vault made in the centre. The body of the great king of the law (Skr. *dharmarāja*) was laid in a composition of loam, silk and paper, placed on a chariot, and to the accompaniment of music interred in the sepulchre. The vault in the interior was entirely filled with treasures, hence the sepulchre became known under the name *Nañ brgyan* ('Having ornaments in the interior'). Five chapels were set up in the interior, and the erection of quadrangular sepulchres took its origin from that time. They are styled *sKu-ri smug-po* ('red grave-mounds')." I. J SCHMIDT (*Geschichte der Ost-Mongolen*, p. 347), translating from *Bodhi-mör*, the Kalmuk version of *rGyal rabs*, erroneously writes the latter name *sMuri*, and makes an image of the king fashioned from clay and buried in the tomb, while the burial of the body is not mentioned. The Kalmuk version is not accessible to me; the Tibetan text is clearly worded as translated above. The same work (fol. 87) imparts the following information on the tomb of King Kʻri-sroñ lde-btsan: "His sepulchre was erected on Mu-ra mountain, in the rear, and to the right, of that of his father. The king had it built during his lifetime. The posthumous name *ạPʻrul ri gtsug snañ* was conferred upon him. At the foot of his sepulchre there is a memorial inscription in stone. The sepulchre became known by the name *Pʻyi rgyan can* ('Ornamented in the exterior')."

1) See *dPag bsam ljon bzañ*, p. 151, l. 25. This term is not explained in our Tibetan dictionaries. The Chinese rendering shows that it is the question of supervising censors.

2) For *bka.*

3) This word is badly mutilated in the stone. The Chinese parallel is *ngo*(*k*), so that I infer Tib. *rñog*, a well-known clan name. The Tibetans have no family names but clan names (Tib. *rus*, Chin. *tsu* 族; compare the account on the Tang-hiang in *Tʻang shu*, ROCKHILL's translation in *The Land of the Lamas*, p. 338) named for the localities from which the clans originated.

4) This lacune corresponds to Tib. *stag*. The character 答 *ta* may be inferred from the name *Lun si ta je* 論悉答熱 (Tib. *Blon stag rje*) in *Tʻang shu* (Ch. 216 下, p. 6a).

*se* ○ *si(k) han*[1]) *k<sup>c</sup>u(t)*. The word *rtsis-pa* was accordingly sounded *tsis-pa*. The Chinese transcription of this ministry (instead of translation as in the preceding cases) indicates that there was no correlate institution for it in China. In the modern administration of Tibet, the *rtsis dpon* had charge of the accounts,[2]) from which it may be inferred that the *rtsis-pa c<sup>c</sup>en-po* of the T<sup>c</sup>ang period had a similar function.

19. *p<sup>c</sup>yi blon ạbro žaṅ* (the remainder is almost destroyed and cannot be positively deciphered) = 紕論沒盧尙 *p<sup>c</sup>i lun mu-lu shang*. The transcription *mu* (compare Japanese *botsu*)-*lu* hints at a pronunciation *bro* for Tib. *ạbro*.

20. *žal-ce-ba*[3]) *c<sup>c</sup>en-po žal-ce* ○ ○ *god* (?) *blon rgyud ṅan li btsan* = 刑部尙書○論結硏歷贊 *hing pu shang shu* ○ *lun kie* (*γ'et*) *ngan* (*yen*) *li tsan*. The transcription of *rgyud* is of importance; it was sounded *g'ut* or *γ'ut*, the prefix *r* being silent.

---

1) Chin. *han*, accordingly, renders Tib. *rgan*, which, after the elimination of the prefix *r*, was presumably sounded *χan*. In a passage of *Yüan shi*, the same Tibetan word is transcribed *han* 罕 (E. v. ZACH, *l. c.*, p. 255). Chin. *h*, therefore, in transcriptions, does not usually correspond to Tib. *h*, but to Tib. *g* with or without prefix. The following case is of especial interest. Tib. *la p'ug*, "radish," is a Chinese loan word derived from *lo p'o* 蘿蔔 (see BRETSCHNEIDER, *Bot. Sin.*, pt. 2, No. 39); consequently also Tib. *guṅ la p'ug*, "carrot," must be the equivalent of Chin. *hu lo p'o* 胡蘿蔔 of the same meaning: so that we obtain the equation Chin. *hu* 胡 (Japanese *ko*) = Tib. *guṅ*. For this reason we are justified in identifying also the name *Hu* 鶻 with Tib. *Guṅ* in the name of the ancestor of the Tibetans mentioned on p. 75, note 4; and *Guṅ rgyal*, as correctly stated by CHANDRA DAS (*Dictionary*, p. 221), according to Tibetan tradition, is the name of one of the early kings of Tibet (the same name occurs also in *Guṅ ri guṅ btsan*, son and successor of King *K'ri-sroṅ*, and in *Spu de guṅ btsan*).

2) ROCKHILL, *J. R. A. S.*, 1891, p. 220.

3) JÄSCHKE writes this word *žal c'e*, which is a secondary development; it is properly *žal lce* ("mouth and tongue"), thus written, for instance, *Avadānakalpalatā* (Tibetan prose ed., p. 71, 7) and CHANDRA DAS (*Dictionary*, p. 1068). The Table (II, 6) offers the spelling *ža-lce*, which, together with the spelling of the inscription, shows that the word was pronounced *žal-ce* in the ninth century. As proved by the Chinese translation 刑, it had, besides the meanings "lawsuit, litigation, judgment," also the significance of "punishment." Tib. *c'en-po*, "the great one," appears as rendering of Chin. *shang shu*.

There are, further, in the inscription, two interesting parallels of geographical names. In line 44 we meet Tib. *stse žuṅ č'eg* (or *ts'eg*) transcribing Chin. *tsiang kün ku* 將軍谷 ("Valley of the General"), and in line 46 Tib. *čeṅ šu hyvan* transcribing Chin. *ts'ing šui hien* 清水縣. The Tibetan word *stse* was pronounced *tsÿ* (the sign *e* including also nasalized *ö*). The addition of the prefixed sibilant *s*- does not prove that this *s* was sounded, but, as in so many other cases, it owes its existence only to the tendency of preserving the high tone which indeed is inherent in the Chinese word *tsiang*. The Tibetan word *tse* without the prefix would have the deep tone, while the prefix indicates that it is to be read in the high tone; the Chinese equivalent *tsiang* (Cantonese *tsöng*, Hakka *tsiong*) undeniably proves that the palatal sibilant was also the initial intended in the Tibetan word. It is entirely out of the question to regard the *s* in *stse* as the articulated initial consonant, and only the desire for regulating the tone can be made responsible for the presence of the prefixed *s*.[1]) We have here, accordingly, unassailable evidence for the fact that the tone system existed in the language of Lhasa at least as early as the first

---

1) An analogous example is presented by Tib. *spar k'a* being a transcription of Chin. *pa kua* 八卦. Chin. **pat, par* (compare Tib. *pir* = Chin. *pit* 筆) never had an initial *s*, and there is no reason whatever why the Tibetans should articulate *spar* a Chinese *par*; of course, they did not, nor do they do so, but say *par*; the unprotected *par*, however, has with them the deep tone, while, if the prefix *s* is superscribed, it receives the high tone, and the high tone is required by the Chinese word; the letter *s* is simply a graphic index of the high tone. Also the high-toned aspirate *k'a* instead of *ka*, which we should expect, seems to be somehow conditioned by the tone of Chin. *kua*. *Vice versa*, Chin. *mo-mo* 饝 ｜ with the even lower tone is written in Tibetan *mog-mog* ("steamed meat-balls"), having likewise the low tone, but not *smog*, which would indicate *mog* in the high tone. — Another interesting loan-word is *lcog-tse* (*rtse*), "table," derived from Chin. *cho(k)-tse* 桌子; the final *g* indicates that the loan is old. The prefix *l* merely has the function of expressing the high tone of the Chinese word; the Tibetans certainly pronounce only *čog-tse* (later spellings are *cog-ts'e* and *cog-ts'o*, the latter in *Li-šii gur-k'aṅ*, fol. 23).

part of the ninth century, and the reason for its coming into existence will immediately be recognized from our general discussion of the phonetic condition of the language in that period. Another interesting example of the presence and effect of tone at that time will be given hereafter in dealing with the word *žaṅ*. Tib. *žuṅ* as equivalent for *kün* 軍 is conceivable only when the Tibetans heard or understood the latter word as *čuṅ* or *šuṅ* with a similar pronunciation, as still existing in the dialects of Wên-chou, Ning-po, and Yang-chou (compare W. *ciung*, N. *cüing*, Y. *chüng*, given in GILES's *Dictionary*); for Tib. *ž* and *j* are regular equivalents of the Chinese palatals *č* and *š* (compare Tib. *kong jo* = Chin. *kung ču* 公主, Tib. *žo* transcribed in Chin. *šo*).[1])

The word *c'eg* (or *ts'eg*) is a Tibetan word, and has nothing to do with Chinese *ku*. The Tibetan transcription *čeṅ* for Chin. *ts'ing* is striking; it is not known to me whether the latter word may have had an initial tenuis in the T'ang period. *Shui* 水 was then doubtless sounded *šu* or *žu*; we shall have to come back to the question why the Tibetan transcription is *šu*. The Tibetan *hyvan* [2]) consists in writing of initial *h* with subscribed *y* (*ya btags*) and following *va zur* which is the semi-vowel *u̯*; phonetically, the word is *h'u̯an*, so that the pronunciation of 縣 must then have been something like the Korean reading *hiön*, or like *hiuan.* [3])

---

1) The case is fully discussed farther on, where more examples will be found.

2) BUSHELL (*l. c.*, p. 105, note *f*) has wrongly printed it *hrun.*

3) It has been asserted that Chin. *Lo sie* 邏些 (*Kiu T'ang shu*, Ch. 196 a, p. 1 b) and *Lo so* 邏娑 (*T'ang shu*, Ch. 216 a, p. 1) are intended to render *Lha-sa*, the capital of Tibet (BUSHELL, *l. c.*, p. 98, note 6; ROCKHILL, *J. R. A. S.*, 1891, p. 190; and CHAVANNES, *Documents*, p. 178). This identification seems to me rather improbable. The Tibetan word *lha* is phonetically *χla*; the initial *χ* is not a prefix which could be dropped, but an integral part of the stem, which is still preserved in all dialects. It is not likely that the form *χla* would be rendered in Chinese exclusively by the one syllable *lo* (formerly *la*, *ra*). The strict reconstruction of *Lo sie* and *Lo so* is *Ra sa*; and *Ra sa* ("Goat's Land"), as is well known, is the ancient name of the city of Lhasa, before it

In connection with this list of Tibetan offices and officials it may be appropriate to examine the designations of the Tibetan Boards of Ministry, as handed down in *Tʻang shu* (Ch. 216 上, p. 1). Not only are the Tibetan names here transcribed, but also their meaning is added in Chinese, so that for the restoration of the Tibetan originals a double test is afforded, — phonetic and semasiological. Nine ministries are distinguished:

1. *lun chʻi* 論茝, styled also *ta lun* 大論 (that is, "great *lun*," Tib. *blon cʻen*) with the meaning 大相, "great minister." BUSHELL (*l. c.*, p. 6) transcribes the title *lunchʻai*, although the Glossary of the *Tʻang shu* (Ch. 23) indicates the reading of the character 茝 as *chʻi* (昌止). From the double interpretation of the term *lun chʻi* it follows that it represents Tib. *blon cʻe*, "great minister."

2. *lun chʻi hu mang* | | 扈莽, styled also *siao lun* 小論 (that is, "small *lun*," Tib. *blon cʻuṅ*) with the meaning 副相, "assistant minister." Chin. *mang* strictly corresponds to Tib. *maṅ*, "many." Chin. initial *h*, as noticed above under No. 18, represents Tib. *g* with or without prefix, and Chin. *u* represents Tib. *o*, so that Chin. *hu*, I am inclined to think, is the equivalent of Tib. *mgo*, "head." In this manner we obtain Tib. *blon cʻe mgo maṅ*, "the many heads (assistants) of the great minister." I have not yet been able to trace this expression in any Tibetan record, but it may turn up some day.

---

received the latter name (CHANDRA DAS, *Dictionary*, p. 1161). The Chinese, as shown by their mode of transcription, were acquainted with the name *Ba-sa*, and perpetuated it even after the change of the name in Tibet. KOEPPEN (*Die lamaische Hierarchie*, p. 332) indicates *Julsung* as a designation of the city after VIGNE, and explains this *yul gsuṅ*, "land of the teaching." This, of course, is impossible: those words could mean only "teaching, or words of the land." But the reconstruction is erroneous: VIGNE's transcription is intended for *yul gžuṅ*, "centre, capital of the land."

3. *si(t) pien ch'ê pu* 悉編掣[1]) 逋 with the significance *tu hu* 都護, "commander-in-chief," corresponding to Tib. *srid*[2]) *dpon c'e-po* (*srid*, "government, ruler, commander;" *dpon*, "master, lord;" *c'e-po*, "the great one"), "the great commander."

4. *nang lun ch'ê pu* 囊論掣逋 with the meaning *nei ta siang* 內大相, "chief minister of the interior," corresponding to Tib. *nań blon* (exactly so in the inscription No. 13) *c'e-po*, "great minister of the interior."[3])

---

1) In the inscription 折.

2) Another explanation is possible. Chin. *si* 悉 is also capable of rendering a Tibetan initial *s-*, when followed by a consonant, as shown by *si lung* 悉弄 = Tib. *sroń* in the name of *K'ri du sroń* mentioned on p. 74. Theoretically we should thus arrive at a Tibetan word **spon* (= Chin. *si pien*), which would represent the equivalent of *dpon*. While this alternation between prefixed *d* and *s* is possible, there is as yet no evidence that *dpon* was also anciently sounded **spon*; but the case deserves consideration, if such a reading should ever occur in an ancient text. Provisionally I therefore prefer to adhere to the restitution *srid dpon*.

3) He is styled also *lun mań je* 論莽熱. The latter word is repeatedly utilized in the inscription to render Tib. *bžer*, which I think is an ancient form of *rje*, "lord." The Tib. *blon mań bžer* or *rje*, accordingly, would mean "the first among the many ministers." This expression appears also as the title of military officers, as in *T'ang shu* (Ch. 216 下, p. 4 b): 南道元帥論莽熱沒籠乞悉笓, "the commander-in-chief of the Southern Circuit *Mo lung k'i si pi* (probably Tib. *Mod sroń k'ri spyi*), with the title *blon mań rje*." *Kiu T'ang shu* imparts only his title without his name. In this respect great caution is necessary, in that the T'ang Annals frequently designate Tibetan officials merely by their titles, not by their names. The commander in question was captured in 802 by Wei Kao, and sent on to the Chinese emperor, who gave him a house to live in. On this occasion it is repeated in *Kiu T'ang shu* (Ch. 196 下, p. 8 b) that *mang je* denotes with the Tibetans the great minister of the interior. The title *mań rje*, indeed, occurs in Tibetan: a contemporary of King *K'ri sroń* was *Sva mań rje gsal* (*dPag bsam ljon bzań*, p. 171), and the son of King *Mań sroń* was *ąDus sroń mań rje* (*ibid.*, p. 150). Analogous titles are *mań sroń*, *mań btsun*, *mań bza* (title of a consort of King *Sroń btsan*). — In the following passage a gloss is imparted for the word *je*. In *T'ang shu* (Ch. 216 下, p. 7 a) mention is made of a general *Shang k'ung je* 尙恐熱, military governor of *Lo mên ch'uan* 落門川, with the family name *Mo* 末, and the name (名) *Nung li je* 農力熱, "which is like the Chinese title *lang* ('gentleman') 猶中國號郎." Chin. *mo* (ancient sounds **mwat* and **mwar*), I am inclined to think, is intended for the Tibetan local and clan name *Mar* or

5. *nang lun mi ling pu* 囊論覔零逋 with the meaning 副相, "assistant minister" (that is, of No. 4). The sound *mi* was anciently *bi* (compare the Japanese reading *beki*). Since the ministers of the interior are divided into three classes, the first and the third of which are designated as "great" and "small," the Chinese transcription *bi-ling-pu* naturally refers to the Tibetan word *ạbriṅ-po*, "the middle one of three." We arrive at the result: Tib. *naṅ blon ạbriṅ-po*, "the middle minister of the interior," or "the minister of middle rank."

6. *nang lun chʿung* 囊論充 with the meaning 小相, "small minister," corresponding to Tib. *naṅ blon cʿuṅ*, "small minister of the interior." 1)

7. *yü χan* (*han*) *po chʿê pu* 喻寒波掣逋 meaning *chêng shi ta siang* 整事大相 (translated by Bushell [*l. c.*, p. 6] "chief

---

*ạBal* (Inscription Nº. 16); the words *nung li je* seem to represent Tib. *luṅ ri rje*, "the lord of valleys and mountains," and it is this Tibetan word *rje* to which the Chinese gloss *lang* refers. The words *shang kʿung je* (Tib. *žaṅ kʿoṅ* [?] *rje*) are certainly not part of the name, but a title. In *Sung shi* (Ch. 492, p. 1) we meet under the year 1020 the title of a Tibetan minister *Lun kʿung je* 論恐熱 (Tib. *blon kʿoṅ* [?] *rje*).

1) It is notable that both Tib. *cʿuṅ* and Chin. 充 agree in tone, which is the high tone. The importance of the tone for Tibeto-Chinese transcriptions is discussed on pp. 79 and 105. — In 751 and 754 the Chinese vanquished Ko-lo-fêng, king of Nan-chao, who took refuge with the Tibetans. These conferred upon him the title *tsan pʿu chung* 贊普鍾, that is, "younger brother of the *btsan-pʿo*" (not *po*, as is always wrongly restored; see the note on this subject farther on), *chung* in the language of the "barbarians" signifying "younger brother." M. Pelliot (*B. E. F. E. O.*, Vol. IV, 1904, p. 158), who has translated this passage, observes, "C'est probablement le *čung* tibétain." This is not quite exact. The Tibetan word here intended is *gcuṅ* (*gčuṅ*, pronounced *čuṅ* in the high tone), the respectful word (*že-sai skad*) for a younger brother (otherwise *nu-bo*), with which Chin. 鍾 exactly harmonizes in sound and tone; this equation (as many other examples in the inscription) proves that the prefixed *g* was not then articulated. The Tibetan word *cʿuṅ* (*čʿuṅ*), "small, young," may denote the younger of two brothers, but cannot be rendered by the Chinese palatal tenuis, only by the aspirate, as proved by the above case Tib. *cʿuṅ*, "small," = Chin. 充 *chʿung*. A Tibetan initial aspirate is regularly reproduced by the corresponding Chinese aspirate.

consulting minister"), corresponding to Tib. *yul*[1]) *rgan-po c'e-po.* Chin. *han* answers to Tib. *rgan*, as we saw in the inscription No. 18; *rgan-po* is still the elder or head man of a village, and the Tibetan term relates to local (*yul*) administration.

8 and 9 do not require any further discussion. They are Tib. *yul rgan ḁbriṅ-po* (Chin. *yü han mi ling pu*), "the middle minister of local administration," and Tib. *yul rgan-po c'uṅ* (Chin. *yü han po ch'ung*), "the small minister of local administration."

These nine Boards are styled collectively *shang lun ch'ê pu t'u kiü* 尙論掣逋突瞿, which is considered by me as a transcription of Tib. *žaṅ blon c'e-po dgu*, "the Nine Great Ministers." The word *žaṅ* is fully discussed on p. 104. The word *t'u* 突 formerly had the initial *d* (Japanese reading *dochi*, Annamese *dout*), the word *kiü* 瞿 had the initial *g* (Japanese *gu*).[2])

The phonetic phenomena to be inferred from the Chinese transcriptions of Tibetan words may be summed up as follows.

We gain an important clew as to the determination of the two vowel signs for *i*, the graphic differentiation of which in the ancient texts has been discussed above (p. 53). The inverted *i*, transcribed by me *i̥*, occurs in four examples: *myi̥ṅ* (= modern *miṅ*) = 名, *p'yi̥* = 紕, *k'ri̥* = 綺立, *zi̥gs* = 昔 *sik.*[3]) Hence it fol-

---

1) Chin. *yü* 喩 = Tib. *yul* occurs likewise in proper names. The *Sung shi* (Ch. 492, p. 2) mentions under the year 991 a governor (折逋 = Tib. *c'e-po*, "great") of Si Liang-chou 西涼州, by name *Ngo yü tan* 阿喩丹, corresponding to Tib. *mṄa* (compare 阿里 = Tib. *mṄa-ri(s)*) *yul brtan*; and under 994 a governor *Yü lung po* 喩龍波, being Tib. *Yul sroṅ-po.*

2) It renders the syllable *go* in *Gotama* (T. WATTERS, *Essays on the Chinese Language*, p. 388), in *Gopāla* (*Life of Hüan Tsang*) and *Suvarṇagotra* (*Memoirs of Hüan Tsang*).

3) A fifth example is afforded by 悉 *sit* transcribing Tib. *srid* in the third Ministerial Board mentioned in *T'ang shu*, and *srid* is written with inverted *i̥* in the sworn treaty of 822 (9—11).

lows that the ancient Tibetan sound *i̥* exactly corresponded to the plain, short Chinese *i*. For the vowel *i* written in the regular modern form we have three examples; namely, *mcʿims* = 琛 *cʿ̣öm*, *rtsis* = 資思 *tse* (*tsi*)-*se*, and *cig* = 市 *ši*. These varying Chinese transcriptions prove that this Tibetan vowel did not sound to the Chinese ear like a definite *i*, but must have been of somewhat indistinct value, something between *i*, *ĭ*, [1]) and *ö*.

The comparison of allied words which Tibetan and Chinese have in common is apt to confirm this result. There are Chinese *sẹ* 四 ("four") corresponding to Tibetan (*b*)*ži*, Chinese *sẹ* 死 ("to die") corresponding to Tibetan *ši*, indicating that Tibetan *i* was an equivalent of this indistinct Chinese vowel *ẹ*. The two Tibetan signs for *i*, therefore, have great significance in the comparative study of Indo-Chinese languages; and their distinction in the ancient monuments must be conscientiously noted and registered, instead of being neglected,[2]) as was done by Mr. Waddell. The inscription of 822 indicates that the two timbres of *i* were still fairly discriminated, but that they were already on the verge of a mutual fusion, as shown by a certain wavering in the employment of the two signs. Thus we find in line 43 *gñis*, but in line 50 *gñi̥s*; in line 43 *kyi̥*, in line 50 *kyi*; and other inconsistencies. Perhaps the phonetic differentiation was already wiped out at that period, and only the graphic distinction upheld on traditional grounds.

---

1) Compare Schaank, *Ancient Chinese Phonetics* (*Tʿoung Pao*, Vol. VIII, 1897, p. 369). — On the other hand, Chin. *i* is rendered by Tib. *e* in the nien-hao *King lung* 景龍 transcribed Tib. *Keṅ luṅ* (in the inscription of 783), probably sounded *Köṅ* (compare *čöṅ kuan* 貞觀 = Tib. *čeṅ kvan* [*ibid.*; accordingly, Tib. *e* = Chin. *ö*]). For this reason it is possible that Chin. *king*, as heard at that time by the Tibetans, was sounded *kʿöng* (compare Korean *kyöng*). Chin. *ti* 帝 (iṇ *huang ti*) is transcribed by Tib. *te* (compare Jap. *tei*, Annamese *de*). *Vice versa*, Tib. *ne* in the inscription (above, Nos. 9 and 13) is rendered by Chin. *ning* (but Hakka *leu*, Korean *yöng*), which, in my opinion, goes to show that Tib. *ne* was nasalized: *nẹ*(*nẽ*) or *nö̦*.

2) The hypothesis of the two *i*'s serving for the distinction of short and long *i* is herewith exploded once for all.

The most signal fact to be gleaned from the Tibeto-Chinese concordances is that phonetic decomposition, which was hitherto regarded as a comparatively recent process of the language, was in full swing as early as the first half of the ninth century. The superscribed and prefixed letters were already mute at that time in the dialect of Lhasa: *blon* was articulated *lon*, *btsan* was *tsan*, *bzaṅ* was *zaṅ*, *bžer* was *žer*, *bka* was *ka*, *lta* was *ta*, *lto* was *to*, *gtogs* was *tog*, *rgyal* was *gyal*, *rgan* was *gan* (probably *χan*); *brtan* was even sounded *tan* 旦. Superscribed *s*, however, seems to have been preserved throughout: the pronunciation of *stang* and *snam* is indicated as *stang* and *snam*, that of *snag* and *stag* as *snag* and *stag*. *P$^c$yi* was sounded *p$^{c}$/i*; the alteration of the palatalized (*mouillé*) labials into palatal *č* and *č$^c$* had apparently not yet taken effect. In the combination of two monosyllables into a unit, the prefix of the second element, when the first terminates in a vowel, was articulated and connected into a syllable with the first element, exactly in the same manner as at present. This is exemplified by the interesting transcription *t$^c$am-t$^c$ung* for Tib. *lta mt$^c$oṅ* (No. 10), which simultaneously proves that the word *mt$^c$oṅ* when isolated was pronounced *t$^c$oṅ*, and by the transcription *ngan pên* for Tib. *mṅa dpon* (No. 16).[1] Compare in recent times the name of the monastery *dGa-ldan*, pronounced *Gan-dan*, hence Chin. *Kan-tan* 甘丹; and Tib. *skye dman* ("woman"), pronounced *kyen* (or *kyer*) *män*, hence transcribed *king mien* 京面 in the Tibetan vocabulary inserted in *T$^c$ao-chou t$^c$ing chi* 洮州廳志, 1907 (Ch. 16, p. 48).

Of final consonants, *d*,[2] *g*, *n*, and *ṅ* were sounded. Final *s* was

---

1) Compare also the above *žaṅ blon c$^c$e dgu*, which, judging from the Chinese mode of transcription, must have been articulated *c$^c$el-gu*.

2) Final *d* was pronounced in *Bod*, as indicated by the transcription 蕃 *pat, pot, pön. It is incorrect, as Mr. ROCKHILL (*J. R. A. S.*, Vol. XXIII, 1901, p. 5) asserts, to say that "the word *Bod* is now, and probably always has been, pronounced like the French *peu*."

sounded when it followed a vowel (*ạdus*), but it was eliminated when following a consonant (*mcʿims* was sounded *cʿim*, *ẓigs* as *zik*).[1])

In regard to final *l*, I feel somewhat doubtful. If my identification of 喩 *yü*, which had no final consonant, with Tib. *yul*, holds good, this would rather indicate that final Tib. *l* was not sounded, or but indistinctly. The transcription 頰 *kiap* (*γ'ap*) for *rgyal* in the inscription No. 11, however, may point to a pronunciation *gyal* (*g'al*, *γ'al*). On the other hand, in the list of royal names in *Tʿang shu* (Ch. 216 上, p. 2a) we find the word *rgyal* rendered by 瘕 *kia* (BUSHELL [*l. c.*, p. 9] transcribes *hsia*; Glossary of *Tʿang shu* 古牙 *ku ya*) in the first of King *Sroṅ btsan*'s an-

---

JÄSCHKE, in the Phonetic Tables of his *Dictionary* (p. XVI), indicates the pronunciation *bhod* for Spiti, *wod* for K'ams, *bhọ'* for Tsang and Ü. In the latter the initial is an aspirate media, and, besides, the word has the deep tone; it has accordingly nothing in common with French *peu*. Mr. ROCKHILL himself (p. 6) indicates that in the tenth and eleventh centuries the sound *peu* was transcribed 不德 *pu-tö* and 孛 (or 伯) 特 *po tʿö*; but surely it was not the sound *peu*, but the sound *bod*, which is clearly enough indicated by these transcriptions. If *bod* was thus sounded in the tenth and eleventh centuries, we are bound to presume that this pronunciation held its ground also in the preceding Tʿang period. Skr. *Bhoṭa* and Ptolemy's Βαῦται afford additional evidence for an ancient indigenous *Bod* sounded *bot*.

1) In final *s* a distinction must be drawn between the suffix -s (called Tib. *yaṅ ạjug*) and radical *s* inhering in the stem. The latter seems to have survived until comparatively recent times, if we may rely upon the transcription 烏思藏 *Wu-se tsang* of the *Ming shi* for Tib. *dBus gTsaṅ* (the two large provinces of Central Tibet); the Chinese equivalent must be based on a Tibetan pronunciation *vus tsaṅ* during the Ming period, while the new transcription 衞 *Wei*, rendering the word *dBus* in the age of the Manchu, clearly indicates that the final phonetic decay resulting in the modern *vui*, *vü*, *'ü*, is an after-Ming event. On the other hand, the name of the temple *bSam-yas* is transcribed *Sam-ye* 三耶 by the Chinese pilgrim Ki-ye in the latter part of the tenth century (CHAVANNES, *B. E. F. E. O.*, Vol. IV, 1904, p. 81, who did not identify this locality; this implies that Ki-ye made his return from India to China by way of Nepal and Tibet). Tib. *yas* is *ya* + *s* of the instrumental case (the temple was fine "beyond imagination," *bsam-yas*); *sam-yä* is still the current pronunciation in Central Tibet (JÄSCHKE, *Tibetan Grammar*, p. 6); but as the ancient pronunciation of 耶 was *ya* (compare 耶婆 *Yava*), it is necessary to assume that Ki-ye, at the time of his sojourn in the famous monastery, heard the pronunciation *Sam-ya*. If he had heard *yas*, he could easily have expressed it by the addition of 悉, as it occurs in 耶悉茗 *yasmin*, "jessamine."

cestors, 瘕悉董摩 *Kia si tung mo*, which I provisionally take as reproducing Tib. *rgyal stoṅ-mo*; further, 夜 *ye* in 弗夜 corresponding to Tib. *Bod rgyal*, "king of Tibet," as title of King *Sroṅ btsan*, and 野 *ye* in 窣勃野 *Su p'o ye* = *Su p'o rgyal*, the Tibetan name and title of Fan-ni, and in 鶻提勃悉野 *Hu* (Tib. *Guṅ*) *t'i* (**de* = Tib. *lde*) *p'o si ye* (= Tib. *rgyal*), the ancestor of the Tibetans. The Chinese symbols employed in these cases, *kia* and *ye*, correspond to an ancient pronunciation **gia* (*γ'a*) (Annamese *gia, ja*), without a final consonant, so that they seem to be indicative of a Tibetan sound *gya'* (*g'a'*, *γ'a*). Final *l* was articulated in the tribal name *Bal-ti* (*rGyal rabs: sbal-ti*), as shown by the Chinese rendering *Pu-lü* 勃律 (CHAVANNES, *Documents*, p. 149), the ancient sounds of this *pu* being **ba* and **b'a* (Ningpo *ba*, Japanese *botsu*, Korean *pal*; it renders the syllable *bha* in Skr. *Bhamātra*), so that *Pu-lü* appears as a reproduction of Tib. *Bal.*[1])

An interesting example of the treatment of Tib. final *l* in Chinese is afforded by the Chinese word *p'êng sha*, "carbonate of soda, natron" (*natrium carbonicum*), which has not yet been explained. Li Shi-chên (*Pên ts'ao kang mu*, 石部, Ch. 11, p. 12) confesses his ignorance in the matter (名義未解); and WATTERS (*Essays on the Chinese Language*, p. 378) is wrong in deriving the Chinese word from Tib. *ba tsa* (to which it has not the slightest similarity), "called also *pen-cha*," which is certainly nothing but the Chinese, and not a Tibetan word. The first and oldest mention of the term, as far as I know, is made in *Kiu Wu Tai shi* (Ch. 138, p. 1b), where *ta p'êng sha* 大鵬砂 ("sand of the great rukh") is enumerated among the products of the T'u-po. This very name is suggestive of being the transcription of a foreign word (the

1) In *T'oung Pao*, 1908, p. 3, *Po-lü* was connected by me with *Bolor*, the ancient name of Baltistān; but *Bolor* seems to be derived from *Bal*.

character 硼 certainly is an artificial formation, the two other characters given by WATTERS are taken from the *Pên tsʻao*). The ancient sounds of the phonetic element *pʻêng* 朋 are **bung*, and the Tibetan word answering in sense to the Chinese is *bul* (JÄSCHKE, *Dictionary*, p. 370), so that Chin. *pʻêng* (*bung*) appears as a reproduction of Tib. *bul*,[1]) simultaneously proving that the final *l* in *bul* was sounded; both words agree also in the low tone.[2])

---

1) Also in the ancient allied words of the two languages, Tib. final *l* corresponds to a final nasal in Chinese: for instance, *dṅul*, "silver" = Hakka *ngyin*, Fukien *ngüng* 銀 (*yin*); Tib. (*s*)*brul*, "snake" = Cantonese and Hakka *mong* 蟒 (*mang*, Jap. *bō*). In other cases Tib. final *g* is the equivalent of Chin. final nasal, as Tib. (*ạb*)*rug*, "dragon" = Chin. *lung* (Jap. *riū*) 龍. But Tib. *buṅ*(*-ba*), "bee" = Chin. *fung* (Korean *pong*) 蜂; Tib. *rṅa-boṅ* (*moṅ*), "camel" = Chin. *pong*, *fong* 峯, "hump of a camel" (Tib. *rṅa* is related to *rṅog*, "hump"); Tib. *maṅ*, "many" = Chin. *mang* 茫 and 厖; Tib. *spyaṅ*(*-ku*), "wolf" = Chin. *mang* 尨 (Korean *pang*, Jap. *bō*), "Tibetan mastiff."

2) On *pʻeng sha* see P. CIBOT (*Mém. conc. les Chinois*, Vol. XI, pp. 343—346); KLAPROTH (*Asiat. Magazin*, Vol. II, pp. 256—261, Weimar, 1802); SOUBEIRAN, *Etudes sur la matière médicale chinoise* (*minéraux*), p. 13 (Paris, 1866); F. DE MÉLY, *Les lapidaires chinois*, p. 141; H. H. HAYDEN, *Geology of the Provinces of Tsang and Ü in Central Tibet* (*Memoirs Geological Survey of India*, Vol. XXXVI, pt. 2, 1907, p. 65). — The Chinese loan-words in Tibetan have not yet been studied, and are hardly indicated in our Tibetan dictionaries. Some of them are even passed off as Sanskrit: for instance, *pi-waṅ* or *pi-baṅ*, "guitar," is said to be derived from Skr. *vīṇā*, which is impossible; in fact, it is to be connected with Chin. 琵琶 *pʻi-pʻa*, ancient sounds **bi-ba* (Japanese *bi-wa*, Mongol *biba*). The nasalization of the final vowel *wa* or *ba* is a peculiarity of Tibetan sometimes practised in foreign words (compare *pi-pi-liṅ*, "pepper" = Skr. *pippalī*). The *Tang hiang* 党項, a Tibetan tribe in the region of the Kukunor, according to *Sui shu* (Ch. 83, p. 8), were in possession of *pʻi-pʻa*; according to Chinese tradition, the instrument originated among the *Hu* 胡, a vague expression generally referring to peoples of Central Asia, Iranians and Turks. GILES (*Biographical Dictionary*, p. 839) ascribes its introduction into China to the Princess of Wu-sun. The Djagatai word for it is *pišik* (*Keleti Szemle*, 1902, p. 161). The fact that the Tibetan and Chinese words refer to the same object is evidenced by the Polyglot Dictionary of Kʻien-lung. In the latter we meet also Tib. *coṅ*, "bell" = Chin. *chung* 鐘. There are, further, Tib. *pʻiṅ*, "pitcher, cup" = Chin. *pʻing* 瓶; Tib. *la-cʻa*, "sealing-wax," from Chin. *la* 蠟, "wax;" Tib. *mog*(*-ša*), "mushroom" = Chin. *mo-ku* 蘑菇; Tib. *tsʻuu* (the double *u* indicates the fourth tone of Chinese), "vinegar" = Chin. *tsʻu* 醋; Tib. *giu* (*gi*)*-waṅ* (*bam*), "bezoar" = Chin. *niu huang* 牛黃 (Jap. *giū-kwō*); Tib. *kau*, "watermelon" = Chin. *kua* 瓜; Tib. *sraṅ*, "ounce" = Chin. *liang* 兩 (Korean *riang*, Jap. *riō*). Tib. *pi-pi*, "flute," and *bid-bid*, "hautboy

On the whole, the probability is greater that the final *l* was

---

reed," must be connected with *pi* 觱 (**bi, bit*; Korean *pʽil*), originally a horn used by the Kʽiang to frighten horses (definition of *Shuo wên*), but then in the compound *pi-li* 觱篥 a pipe (A. C. MOULE, *Chinese Musical Instruments, J. Ch. Br. R. A. S.*, 1908, p. 84), in *Huang chʽao li kʽi tʽu shi* (Ch. 9, p. 53) figured and described as a reed flute with three holes, metal mouthpiece and broadening funnel, 5.37 inches long, used for dance music by the Turkish tribe *Warka* 瓦爾喀. The word, therefore, is presumably of Turkish origin, but it is much older than the eighteenth century. We meet it in the transcription *pei-li* 貝蠡 in the chapter on music in *Kiu Tʽang shu* (Ch. 29, p. 8 b), where it is defined as a copper horn 銅角, two feet long, of the shape of an ox-horn, in use among the Western Jung 西戎. According to another tradition, it originated in Kucha, Turkistan (*Ko chi king yüan*, Ch. 47, p. 6 b). The original Turkish form seems to have been *beri* or *böri* (H. VÁMBÉRY, *Die primitive Cultur des turko-tatarischen Volkes*, p. 145, notes a word *boru*, "trumpet," properly "reed"); and we find this word in Mongol *böriyä*, "trumpet," from which Manchu *buren* and *buleri* seem to be derived. The latter corresponds in the Polyglot Dictionary to Chin. *la-pa* 喇叭, Mongol *ghūlin böriyä*, "brass trumpet," and Tib. *zaṅs duṅ*. The Mongol word *rapal* given in the first edition of GILES, and repeated by MOULE, does not exist (Mongol has neither initial *r* nor a *p*); nor can Chin. *la-pa* be derived from Manchu *laba*, as stated in the second edition, the latter being merely a transcript of Chinese, as already pointed out by SACHAROV. *La-pa* is neither Mongol nor Tibetan; it is listed among the musical instruments of Turkistan in *Hui kiang chi* 回疆誌 (Ch. 2, p. 8), published 1772 (WYLIE, Notes, p. 64). The musical instrument *kan tung* 干動, left unexplained by MOULE (*l. c.*, p. 103), is Tib. *rkaṅ duṅ*, the well-known trumpet made from a human thigh-bone; I met also the transcription 剛洞. Among the interesting loan-words of cultivated plants, we have Tib. *se-qbru* (pronounced *se-ru*), "pomegranate" (*punica granatum* L.), derived from Chin. 石榴 *shi-liu*, anciently *se(shĭ)-ru* (Japanese *-ro*). The pomegranate does not thrive in Tibet, and, as is well known, was introduced into China by General Chang Kʽien (BRETSCHNEIDER, *Bot. sin.*, pt. 1, p. 25; pt. 3, No. 280; HIRTH, *Tʽoung Pao*, Vol. VI, 1895, p. 439; *Pên tsʽao kang mu* 果部, Ch. 30, p. 8). Whether Chin. *ru, ro*, is connected with Greek *ῥοά* or Arabic *rummān*, Amharic *rūmān* (SCHRADER in HEHN, Kulturpflanzen und Haustiere, 8th ed., p. 247), I do not venture to decide. The Tibetan word must be regarded as a loan from Chinese, and not as indigenous, as W. SCHOTT (*Entwurf einer Beschreibung der chinesischen Litteratur*, p. 123, note, Berlin, 1854) was inclined to believe, who explained the word as being composed of Tib. *se*, "rose," and *qbru*, "grain, seed." These Tibetan words (the meanings "pomegranate" and "rosebush" interchange in South-Slavic) were doubtless chosen as elements of the transcription, because they conveyed to the national mind some tangible significance with reference to the object (in the same manner as there are numerous analogous cases in the Chinese transcriptions of foreign words). The Central-Tibetan pronunciation *sen-ḍu* and Ladākhi *sem-ru* represent secondary developments suggested by the mode of spelling, and application of phonetic laws based thereon (nasalization of the prefix *q*, transcribed *ṅeŋ* 恩 in *Hua i yi yü*).

articulated than that it was suppressed, and the same remark holds good of final *r*. For the latter we have the only example in the word *bžer*, transcribed by Chin. *že* (Nos. 10, 13—15, above). In this case the Chinese transcription certainly is not conclusive, since Chinese lacks final *r*, and, taking into consideration that the other finals were heard, there seems good reason to assume that *bžer* was pronounced *žer* at that period.

The subjoined *r* was still clearly sounded in the guttural and labial series. The word *k$^c$ri*, as evidenced by the Chinese transcription *k$^c$i-li*, 1) was actually heard as *k$^c$ri* (not as at present, *t$^c$i*);

---

Lolo *sebuma* (P. VIAL, *Dict. français-lolo*, p. 176, Hongkong, 1909) possibly points to a former Tibetan articulation *seb-ru*.

1) The T$^c$ang Annals employ various methods of transcribing the word *k$^c$ri* ("throne") in the beginning of the names of the Tibetan kings, 乞黎, 乞立, 棄隸 (*k$^c$i li*), and also only 棄 and 器 (*k$^c$i*). Probably also *k$^c$o* (*ka*) *li* 可黎 in the name *K$^c$o li k$^c$o tsu* 可黎可足 (being identical with the Tibetan king K$^c$ri-lde sroṅ-btsan) is the equivalent of Tib. *k$^c$ri*. The Chinese rendering of his name has not yet been explained. The elements *lde sroṅ btsan*, the Chinese equivalents of which are well known to us, cannot be made responsible for Chin. *k$^c$o tsu* (ancient sounds *ka tsuk*). In *rGyal rabs* this king is designated also *K$^c$ri gtsug lde btsan Ral-pa-can*; so that we are bound to assume that the Chinese name *K$^c$o-li ka-tsuk* is intended for the first two elements of this Tibetan name, *K$^c$ri gtsug*. It is singular, however, at first sight, that in this case the prefixed *g* is expressed by the Chinese syllable *k$^c$o* (*ka*), while in another royal name Tib. *gtsug* is transcribed in Chinese regardless of the prefix (see p. 92, note 2). The Tibetan prefix is often preserved in the second element of a compound if the first word terminates in a vowel; the words *k$^c$ri gtsug* could be sounded *k$^c$rik-tsug*, and hence the Chinese mode of transcription. The case is analogous to that of *lta mt$^c$oṅ* pointed out on p. 86. An interesting Chinese transcription of a Tibetan word showing the preservation of *r* is the word *p$^c$u-lu* 氆氌, "woollen cloth," a reproduction of Tib. *p$^c$rug*. As far as I know, the Chinese term does not occur in the T$^c$ang period, but only from under the Yüan. The mode of writing (Manchu *p$^c$uru*) presupposes a Tibetan pronunciation *p$^c$ru'*, for the phonetic element *lu* 魯 is devoid of a final consonant. In the age of the T$^c$ang, when the word sounded *p$^c$rug* also in the dialect of Lhasa, a complement sounding *luk*, for instance 祿, would have doubtless been chosen in forming the second character in the word. The very mode of transcription thus betrays a post-T$^c$ang origin, but it must result from a time when the initials *p$^c$r* were still in full swing and had not yet undergone the *lautverschiebung* into the cerebrals *t$^c$r*, *t$^c$* (see also KLAPROTH, *Description du Tubet*, p. 50, Paris, 1831; T. WATTERS, *Essays on the Chinese Language*, p. 378).

*kru* (*kū-li*) was sounded *kru*; the word *ḥbro* (No. 19) was sounded *bro*, and *ḥbriṅ*, as shown by the Chinese transcription *bi-liṅ*, was articulated *briṅ*, [1]) and *blo* was *blo*. In the combination *sr*, the *r* seems to have been dropped, if the identification of 悉 *sit* in *T*$^{c}$*ang shu* with Tib. *srid* holds good.[2])

---

1) Another good example of the initials *br* being sounded with perfect clearness is presented by the word 拂廬 *fu-lu* (**bu-ro*), imparted in the T$^{c}$ang Annals as a gloss for the Tibetan word meaning "a felt tent." The word intended apparently is Tib. *sbra*, "felt tent," still sounded *bra* in western Tibet and so likewise in the T$^{c}$ang period. The Chinese syllable *bu* reproduces the initial *b*, and the syllable *lu* the Tib. *ra*. It is strange, however, that the Chinese did not choose in this case an element *ra*, *la*; but this may be easily accounted for by the fact that the above Chinese word *lu* means "a hut, a hovel," and also the tent erected for the wedding ceremony. As in so many other cases, the Chinese selected a word approximately imitative of the foreign sound, and simultaneously indicative of the significance of the foreign word. The Tibetan word *gur*, "tent," can certainly not be sought in the Chinese transcription, as 拂 never had the sounds *gu* or *ku*. A good modern example of Chinese rendering of Tib. *br* is 老木郎 = Tib. *Lha-braṅ*; in this compound the second element is still pronounced *braṅ* (but never *ḍaṅ*) throughout Tibet, while *p*$^{c}$*o-braṅ*, "palace," is always *p*$^{c}$*o-ḍaṅ*. These two elements *braṅ*, therefore, seem to be two words of different origin.

2) But the word *sroṅ* in the names of several kings was doubtless articulated *sroṅ*, as evidenced by the transcriptions in the T$^{c}$ang Annals 宗 (*tsung*; Japanese *sō*, *su*) 弄 (*lung*), *si lung* 悉弄, *su lung* 蘇籠 and *si lung* 悉籠. Mr. ROCKHILL (*The Life of the Buddha*, p. 211) is inclined to think that Chin. *K*$^{c}$*i tsung lung tsan* renders Tib. *K*$^{c}$*ri ldan sroṅ btsan*; but Chin. *tsung* cannot reproduce Tib. *ldan* (pronounced *dan*). In my opinion, the Chinese words are intended only for *K*$^{c}$*ri sroṅ btsan*. In regard to the name of King *K*$^{c}$*i li̦ so tsan* 棄隸蹜贊, Mr. ROCKHILL (p. 217) takes it as "giving a quite correct pronunciation of the four first syllables of his Tibetan name," that is, *K*$^{c}$*ri lde gtsug btsan*. But Chin. *li* cannot represent an equivalent of Tib. (*l*)*de*, which, as pointed out on p. 74, is rendered by Chin. *lie* 獵. The Chinese words exactly reproduce the Tibetan words *K*$^{c}$*ri* (*g*)*tsug* (*b*)*tsan*. The character 蹜 is sounded in Cantonese *shuk*, Korean *suk*, *č*$^{c}$*uk*, Japanese *shuku*, and seems to have had in the T$^{c}$ang period the value of **tsuk*, **dzuk*. BUSHELL (*The Early History of Tibet*) unfortunately availed himself of the Wade system in the transcription of Tibetan names, so that they are useless for the purpose of identification, and wrote names sometimes consisting of five and six syllables into one solid word without divisions, which led his successors into error; for instance, HERBERT MUELLER (*Tibet in seiner geschichtlichen Entwicklung*, *Z. f. vergl. Rechtswissenschaft*, Vol. XX, p. 325), who transcribes *Ch'in-u-hsi-lung* instead of *K*$^{c}$*i nu si lung*. An error of transcription was committed by BUSHELL (pp. 5, 39) in the name written by him after *Kiu T*$^{c}$*ang shu Sohsilunglichtsan* (and so repeated by ROCKHILL, p. 219, and MUELLER, *l. c.*), where *P*$^{c}$*o* (婆, confounded with

Initial and final consonants, in general, were still intact, but prefixed consonants were doomed to being silent. It it natural that tones began to be developed in consequence of this phonetic disintegration (p. 79); for we know, particularly from CONRADY's researches,

---

婆) *si lung lie tsan* (corresponding to Tib. *P$^c$o sroṅ lde btsan*) must be read. The *T$^c$ang shu* (Ch. 216 上, p. 8a) writes the same name 挲悉籠臘贊 *So* (ancient sound *sa*) *si lung la tsan*; nevertheless BUSHELL's *So si lung lie tsan* remains inexact, as we have either *P$^c$o si lung lie tsan* of the *Kiu T$^c$ang shu* or *So si lung la tsan* of the *T$^c$ang shu.* The latter spelling, however, is erroneous. The historical observation inserted by Mr. ROCKHILL shows that this is a case of importance, as, according to him, this name has not yet been traced in Tibetan history. But if names are wrongly transcribed and inexactly restored, any attempt at identification is naturally hopeless at the outset. All the Tibetan words and names encountered in the T$^c$ang Annals are capable of rigorous philological research; and when this is properly carried through, much of the alleged diversity between Chinese and Tibetan traditions (BUSHELL, p. 4) will be blown up into the air. Mr. ROCKHILL's conclusion that in the *T$^c$ang shu* the king *So si lung lie tsan* is inserted between *K$^c$i li so tsan* and *K$^c$i li tsan*, whereas all Tibetan histories are unanimous in affirming that *K$^c$ri sroṅ* succeeded his father on the throne, is not at all to the point; likewise BUSHELL (p. 5) is wrong in making *So si lung lie tsan* and *K$^c$i li tsan* two individuals and two different kings. They designate, indeed, one and the same personage, who is none other than the Tibetan king *K$^c$ri sroṅ lde btsan.* This name appears in both *T$^c$ang shu* as that of the king who died in 755 (BUSHELL, p. 39), but this is the same king previously styled *K$^c$i li so tsan* (*K$^c$ri gtsug btsan*), so that it is evident beyond cavil that it is simply a clerical error which here crept in when the annalist copied from his state documents. It was *K$^c$ri gtsug btsan* who died in that year; and it was his son *K$^c$ri sroṅ lde btsan* who succeeded to him, and who was styled — the annalist meant or ought to say — also *P$^c$o sroṅ.* This reading of *Kiu T$^c$ang shu* is doubtless correct, whereas the *so* of the New Annals must be a clerical error. Tib. *p$^c$o,* "the male," is an ancient title occurring in the names of the Tibetan kings, as will be seen below in a discussion of the word *btsan-po,* which had originally the form *btsan p$^c$o,* "the warlike one, the male." Likewise *rgyal-po,* "the king," was originally *rgyal p$^c$o,* "the victorious male" (compare WADDELL, *J. R. A. S.*, 1909, p. 1268, whose explanation is certainly a fantasy; the title *p$^c$o* implies nothing derogatory). It is worthy of note that also the chief consort of the king, *P$^c$o yoṅ* (or *γyoṅ*) *bza,* bore the title *p$^c$o* in her name, whereas his other wives were not entitled to this privilege. In the transcription 勃弄若 *P$^c$o lung* (BUSHELL, p. 9, *mung*) *jo* (= Tib. *žo*) the same title *P$^c$o sroṅ* appears in the name of the fifth of King *Sroṅ btsan*'s ancestors (*T$^c$ang shu*, Ch. 216 上, p. 2 a). The title *P$^c$o rgyal* occurs in the name 窣勃野 *Su p$^c$o ye* (**gia*), adopted by Fan Ni 樊尼 on his election as king of the T$^c$u-fa (BUSHELL, p. 6), and in the name of the ancestor 祖 of the T$^c$u-po, 鶻提勃悉野 *Hu* (Tib. *guṅ*) *t'i* (Tib. *lde*) *p'u* (Tib. (*p$^c$o*) *si* (possibly Tib. *srid*) *ye* (Tib. *rgyal*) = Tib. *Guṅ* (see p. 78) *lde p$^c$o srid rgyal.*

that tones are the substitutes of eliminated consonants. Presuming that writing, when introduced in the first half of the seventh century, rather faithfully fixed the condition of the language as then spoken, we are confronted by the fact that the first stage in the process inaugurating the remarkable phonetic decomposition of the Tibetan language took place within a period of hardly a century and a half. In the first part of the ninth century a deep gulf was yawning between the methods of writing and speaking, and due regard must be taken of this fact in our studies of the manuscripts of that epoch. The natural tendency of writing words in the same manner as they came from the lips of the speakers was then steadily growing. The inscription of 822 (above, No. 17) furnishes a curious example in writing the word *bka* with the single letter *k*, which, even more than the Chinese transcription *kia*, is undubitable proof that it was sounded simply *ka*.[1])

---

1) For the present I refrain from a discussion of the laws underlying the Chinese method of transcribing Tibetan words, as several intricate points remain to be cleared up. It will be observed that this method in some respects differs from what we are wont to have in the case of Sanskrit, Turkish, and Persian transcriptions, and that in the face of Tibetan the Chinese were compelled to struggle with difficulties which they did not encounter in other foreign languages. It is manifest that the Chinese transcriptions, as we have them now, were recorded at the time when the decomposition of the Tibetan prefixes and initials had set in, and when the tone system sprang into existence. The tones could not escape the Chinese ear, and were bound to influence their manner of transcribing. The fact that the new initials were affected by the eliminations of the prefixed consonants, most of which were grammatical elements of formative functions, is evident from what we observe in the modern dialects; thus far, however, we are not in a position to frame any definite conclusions in regard to such changes during the ninth century. Nevertheless they must have taken place, as we see from several parallels in the inscription of 822. Whereas all the Tibetan true initial aspirates are exactly reproduced by the corresponding Chinese aspirate, we notice that Chinese has an aspirate where Tibetan offers a tenuis + silent prefix; for instance, Tib. *(l)ta* = Chin. $t^{c}an$ 貪 (No. 10), and Tib. *(l)to* = Chin. $t^{c}u$ 土 (No. 14). Whether Tib. *t* was really aspirated or changed into the aspirate media $d^{c}$, I do not venture to decide; but the Chinese transcriptions are a clear index of the fact that the tenuis had undergone some sort of revolution prompted by the elision of the prefixed *l*. In other instances, judging from

## Phonology of Document Pelliot.

We now enter into a discussion of the phonology of the text of *document Pelliot.* M. Bacot himself has noted the addition of

---

the Chinese transcriptions, the tenuis remained unaffected; as, *gtogs* = *tuk* 篤, *brtan* = *tan* 旦. This case is of importance when we meet Tibetan names in the Chinese annals and are intent on restoring them to their original forms. Take, for instance, the name of the king 陀土度 *Tʿo tʿu tu(k)* (*Tʿang shu*, Ch. 216 上, p. 2 a), the second in the series of the ancestors of King *Sroṅ btsan.* At first sight, I felt much tempted to recognize in the first two elements the Tib. *tʿo tʿo* occurring in the name of King *Lha tʿo tʿo ri* of Tibetan tradition, but due regard paid to the case just cited makes me skeptical: the Chinese dental aspirate may correspond to this sound in Tibetan, but it may express also Tib. *lt* (hence also *rt*, and probably *st*). Since 土 in the inscription is the equivalent of *lto*, it may very well be that this is the case also in the above name, which may be restored *Tʿo lto bdag* (度 **dak*; Japanese *taku*, *do*; Korean *tʿak*). This consideration has a bearing also on the interpretation of the tribal name 吐蕃 *Tʿu po (fan)*, the second element of which has correctly been identified with Tib. *bod*; for the first element, Tib. *stod*, "upper," and *mtʿo*, "high," have been proposed (the various theories are clearly set forth by L. Feer, *Étymologie, histoire, orthographe du mot Tibet*, *Verh. VII. Or.-Congr.*, pp. 68—81; and Yule and Burnell, *Hobson-Jobson*, p. 917). The first objection to be raised to these identifications is that they are merely based on guesswork, and not on any actual name of Tibet found in Tibetan records. Neither in *rGyal rabs* nor in any other Tibetan history did I ever come across such a name as *stod bod* or *mtʿo bod*, but Tibet and Tibetans are simply called *Bod*, with or without the usual suffixes. It is true, Mr. Rockhill (*J. R. A. S.*, 1891, p. 5) is very positive in his assertion that "Tibetans from Central Tibet have at all times spoken of that portion of the country as *Teu-Peu* (*stod bod*) or 'Upper Tibet,' it being along the upper courses of the principal rivers which flow eastward into China or the Indian Ocean" (in his *The Life of the Buddha*, p. 216, he still adhered to the fanciful *tʿub-pʿod* etymology of Schiefner), but no documentary evidence for this statement is presented; and, as long as such is not forthcoming, I decline to believe in such invented geographical names as *stod bod* and *mtʿo bod*, alleged to have resulted in the Chinese word *Tʿu-po* of the Tʿang period. From a philological point of view, it is entirely impossible to restore Chin. *tʿu* 吐 to Tib. *stod*, for in the same manner as its phonetic element 土, it was never provided with a final consonant; it may be restored to a Tib. *tʿo*, *lto* or *sto* (*mtʿo* seems very doubtful). The Tʿang Annals impart an alleged older name 禿髮 *Tʿu-fa*, which was subsequently corrupted 語訛 into *Tʿu-po*. Mr. Rockhill (*l. c.*, p. 190) comments on this name that "the old sound of *fa* in *Tʿu-fa* was *bat* or *pat*; consequently *Tʿu-fa* represents *Teu-peu* (*stod bod*), our Tibet." I regret being unable to follow this demonstration; *tʿu* cannot represent *tö*, and *pat* does not represent *bod*. The word *tʿu* 禿 was anciently possessed of a final *k*, so that we have *tʿuk pat*, which certainly has nothing to do with *stod bod* or *mtʿo bod*, or anything like it. It is clearly indicated in the Tʿang Annals that the word *Tʿu-fa* the subscribed letter *y* after *m* when followed by the vowels *e* or *i*. We find here *myed* = *med*, "there is not;" *bud-myed* = *bud-med*, "woman;" [1]) *mye* = *me*, "fire;" *myi* = *mi*, "man;" *myi* =

---

(apparently a nickname) was not of Tibetan origin, but derived from Li Lu-ku 利鹿孤 of the Southern Liang dynasty and carried over to the K'iang tribes by his son Fan Ni 樊尼. The name *T'u-fa*, accordingly, is not capable of restitution into Tibetan, and the alleged change of the tribal name from *T'uk-pat* into *T'u-pot* is merely inspired by a certain resemblance of these names. Nor can the Arabic designation تبت of Iṣṭakhri, Khordādba, etc., which has been variously spelled Tobbat, Tibbat, etc., be set in relation with this alleged *T'u(k)-pat*, as only the consonants are expressed by Arabic writing, and the vowels are optional; it offers no valid proof for the attempt at restoring the original Tibetan form, but it shows in the case of Iṣṭakhri that a name for Tibet with the consonants *Tbt* existed toward the end of the sixth century. *T'u-po* must be regarded as the correct and original tribal designation; but as to the proper Tibetan equivalent of 吐, we have to await thorough evidence. It is hoped that a Tibetan gloss for it will turn up in some *document Pelliot*. — The identification of Tibetan proper names in the T'ang annals with those of the Tibetan annals is beset with difficulties, as many names of the Chinese annals are not mentioned by the Tibetans or given by them in a form not identical with the Chinese. The famous minister *mGar*, as already recognized by ROCKHILL (*The Life of the Buddha*, p. 216), is identical with *Lu tung tsan* 祿東贊 with the name *Kü* 婁氏 in *Kiu T'ang shu* (BUSHELL, *l. c.*, p. 12). Theoretically I should restore *Lu tung tsan* to Tib. *Lug stoṅ btsan*, but *rGyal rabs* has preserved to us this name in the form *Se le stoṅ btsan* (SCHMIDT, *Geschichte der Ost-Mongolen*, p. 359, transcribes according to *Bodhi-mör*: *Ssele sDong bDsan*); *Se le*, nevertheless, cannot be the model of Chin. *lu(k)*. *Lu tung tsan* had five sons, — *T'san si jo* 贊悉若, *K'in ling* 欽陵 (perhaps Tib. *dKon gliṅ*), *Tsan p'o* 贊婆 (Tib. *bTsan-p'o*), *Si to kan* 悉多干, *Po lun* 勃論 (Tib. *Po-blon*). The third and fifth are not names, but mere titles. In *rGyal rabs* (fol. 77) I find only two sons of the minister mentioned, — *gÑa* (in another passage *sÑan*) *btsan ldem-bu* and *sTag-ra k'oṅ lod*. Except the element *btsan*, there is nothing in these names that could be identified with any part of the Chinese transcriptions.

1) The word *bud-med* has been interpreted by A. SCHIEFNER (*Mélanges asiatiques*, Vol. I, p. 358) as meaning "the powerless one" (*die kraftlose*) on the mere assumption that the element *bud* has developed from *bod*, and that *bod* is a *verdünnung* of the verb *p'od*, "to be able, capable," which, according to him, holds good also for the word *Bod*, "Tibet." These far-fetched etymologies are based on a now outgrown view of things phonetic. The vowel *u* has not arisen from *o* owing to *trübung*, as assumed by SCHIEFNER, nor is there anything like a *schwächung* of an aspirate sound to a media. *Bud*, *bod*, and *p'od* are three co-existing, distinct matters of independent valuation, and without mutual phonetic relationship. There is no phonetic law to connect them. The whole explanation is not prompted by any rigorous application of phonology, but doubtless inspired by the

*mi*, "not;" *dmyig* = *mig*, "eye." The same phenomenon has been observed in the fragments of the *Çālistambasūtra* found by A. Stein (*Ancient Khotan*, Vol. I, pp. 549, 564; observations of BARNETT and FRANCKE) and in the inscription of King K'ri-sroṅ lde-btsan of the year A. D. 783 (WADDELL, *J. R. A. S.*, 1909, p. 945). [1]) These authors merely point out this case as an instance of archaic orthography, as also M. BACOT speaks of "certains archaïsmes de graphie et d'orthographe." But it should be understood that this peculiar way of writing naturally corresponds to a phonetic phenomenon; the subjoined letter *y* (called in Tibetan *ya btags*) indicates the palatalization of the consonant to which it is attached. How this process came about is easily to be seen in the case of the negative copula *myed*, formed of the negation *ma* + the copula *yod*, yielding *myöd*, in phonetic writing *m'öd*. The letter *e* covers

---

Sanskrit word *abalā* given as a synonym of the word "woman" in *Amarakosha* (ed. *Bibl. ind.*, p. 140). But we only have to cast our eyes on the Tibetan version to see that *abalā* corresponds, not to Tib. *bud-med*, but to Tib. *stobs-med*, while Tib. *bud-med* appears as equivalent of Skr. *strī*. Consequently Skr. *abalā* cannot be made responsible for Tib. *bud-med*; there is no relation between the two; Tib. *stobs-med* is an artificial rendering of Skr. *abalā*. The main objection to be raised to SCHIEFNER's etymology, however, is that it flatly contradicts the natural facts. The Tibetan woman is very far from being weak or without strength, but is physically well developed, — an observation made by all travellers, nor did it escape the Chinese writers on Tibet. "Tibetan women are robust and the men weak, and one may frequently see women performing in the place of their husbands the socage services which the people owe" (ROCKHILL, *J. R. A. S.*, 1891, p. 230). It is not necessary to expand on this subject, but "the weak sex" would be applicable in Tibet only to man. A more plausible explanation of the word may now be offered. It was, of course, doubtful whether the second element *med* was really identical with the negative copula *med*; it may have been, after all, a different word. But the old form *bud-myed* confirms the opinion that this *med* has arisen from *myöd*, *ma yod*. In the first element the word *bu* ("child, son;" *bu-mo*, "girl, daughter") may clearly be recognized, and *bud* (as other monosyllables terminating in *d*) is a contraction of *bu* + *yod*, "the condition of being a child or girl." *Bud-med*, accordingly, means "one who is no longer a girl, an adult woman," and in this sense the word is indeed utilized.

1) It occurs likewise in the inscription of 822, presenting the interesting example *myiṅ rus*. As has been pointed out, this expression is employed on the same occasion in *rGyal rabs* in the form *miṅ rus*, so that the identification of *myiṅ* with *miṅ* is absolutely certain.

also the vocalic timbre *ö*.[1]) The word *myi* accords in sound with Russian мы.[2])

This alternation between hard and palatalized consonants, restricted to the guttural and labial series and to dental *n*, is still conspicuous in the modern language, and has already been noted by A. SCHIEFNER in his "Tibetische Studien."[3]) As to *m*, SCHIEFNER refers to the pairs *miṅ* — *myiṅ*, "name;" *mid* — *myad*, "gullet;" *smig* — *smyig*, "reed." He correctly compares Tib. *mig*, "eye," with Burmese *myak*, and he also knows that the older forms *myed* and *myin* have been preserved along with *med* and *min*; there are such alternations as *k*$^c$*em* — *k*$^c$*yem*, *k*$^c$*ab* — *k*$^c$*yab*, *gon* — *gyon*, *ḍbo* — *ḍbyo*, *p*$^c$*e* — *p*$^c$*ye*, *nag* — *ñag*, *rnil* — *rñil*, and many others. In Ladāk and Lahūl we find the labial tenues, aspirates and mediae, where the written language offers the corresponding palatalized sounds, as may be gleaned from the Phonetic Table preceding JÄSCHKE's *Dictionary* (p. XVIII) and F. B. SHAWE.[4])

The verb *gsod*, "to kill," appears as *sod* without the prefix twice (Table II, 8; VI, 2) and with it once (XI, 3), which indicates that the spelling was as vacillating at that time as it is now.[5]) The stem of the verb is *sad* (Ladākhi *sat*), as shown also by Burmese *sat* and Chinese *šat* 殺. Likewise we have *toṅ* in lieu of *gtoṅ* in V. 7. Also in this case the stem is *taṅ* or *toṅ*.[6])

1) This is best attested by the Tibetan transcription *ceṅ* (*čeṅ*) of Chin. *čöṅ* 貞 (in the nien-hao *Chêng-kuan*) in the inscription of 788 (WADDELL, *J. R. A. S.*, 1909, p. 950, l. 29; the writing *ceṅ ṅa kvan* must be due to a slip in copying the text of the inscription).

2) The Chinese transcriptions assist us again. Compare above under No. 20 Tib. *rgyud* = Chin. *g'ut*, *γ'ut*.

3) *Mélanges asiatiques*, Vol. I, pp. 370—371.

4) *J. A. S. B.*, Vol. LXIII, pt. 1, 1894, p. 12.

5) LAUFER, *Ein Sühngedicht der Bonpo*, *l. c.*, p. 21.

6) Compare such cases as occurring in the inscription, *mt*$^c$*oṅ* sounded *t'oṅ*, *gtogs* sounded *tog*, etc.

These spellings cannot therefore be explained as irregularities or negligence on the part of the writer. From a grammatical standpoint they are perfectly legitimate, for the prefixes *g* and *b* are purely formative elements indicating tenses of the verb. The Tibetan grammarians are fully conscious of this process, as shown by me on a former occasion;[1] the prefix *b* denotes the past and the active, the prefixes *g* and *d* the present, the prefix *ḁ* the passive and future, the prefix *m* an invariable state.

The prefix *r* is omitted in *bda* = *brda* (V. 5), the prefix *ḁ* in *ts͑o ts͑o* (V. 9), the prefix *d* (or *r*) in *mu* (V. 15). We accordingly meet symptoms of simplified spelling prompted, as we saw above, by the phonetic conditions prevailing at that time.

The prefix *l* appears in *lteṅ* (V. 6, 24) in the place of *s* (*steṅ*); compare *ldib-pa* and *sdib-pa*, *lṅa*, "five," in Ladākhi *šṅa*, *lga* and *sga*, "ginger," *lbu-ba* and *sbu-ba*, "bubble."

The sound *n* in lieu of *l* appears in *nam naṅs*, "daybreak," for the normal *nam laṅs*. Schiefner[2] has pointed out the same form in the *ḁDsaṅs-blun* (where also *laṅs* occurs), and considers both forms as equally legitimate.

In Table I, 6, we meet the word *me-tog*, "flower," in the form *men-tog*, which, according to Jäschke, still occurs in the West Tibetan dialects; but it is heard also in eastern Tibet. Mr. Barnett[3] has pointed out the form *me-t͑og* in the fragments of the *Çālistambasūtra*, and, as the *m* is not palatalized, arrays it as an exception among the palatalized *m*. The assumption that *men* presents the older form may account for the preservation of the hard *m*.

Of great interest is the form *nam-ka*, "heaven" (Table I, 9),

1) *Studien zur Sprachwissenschaft der Tibeter*, pp. 529, 548.

2) *Ergänzungen und Berichtigungen zu Schmidt's Ausgabe des Dsanglun*, p. 9, St. Pet., 1852.

3) *Ancient Khotan*, p. 549.

which occurs also once in the fragments of the *Çālistambasūtra* found by A. Stein (*Ancient Khotan*, p. 555), while in other cases it is written *nam-mk<sup>c</sup>a*. This case is of importance, because the word has been looked upon as a loan from Sanskrit. O. BOEHTLINGK [1]) was the first to entertain this opinion. W. SCHOTT [2]) explained *namk<sup>c</sup>a* as developed from *nabk<sup>c</sup>a*, "since evidently it has arisen from the combination of two Sanskrit synonyms for 'air' and 'heaven,' *nab<sup>c</sup>as* and *k<sup>c</sup>a*." In a rather dogmatic form the same question is taken up again by Mr. WADDELL, [3]) who makes the statement, "For the conception of heaven in the Indian and Western sense the Tibetans use the word *mk<sup>c</sup>a*, which they clearly borrowed from the Sanskrit *k<sup>c</sup>a*, as they evidently had no indigenous word of their own to express it." The somewhat generous application of "clearly" and "evidently" does not appeal to everybody; what is evident to one is not always so to another, as opinions largely vary on the nature and quality of evidence. The *Kiu T<sup>c</sup>ang shu* (Ch. 196 上, p. 1) informs us that the shamans of the Tibetans invoke the gods of Heaven and Earth (令巫者告于天地), and that in the prayer during sacrifice the spirit of Heaven 天神 is implored. [4]) If the Tibetan shamans invoked the deity of Heaven, they must "evidently" have possessed a word by which to call it; and that

---

1) In his article *Ueber eine tibetische Uebersetzung des Amarakosha* (*Bull. de l'Acad. de St. Pétersbourg*, Vol. III, No. 14, pp. 209—219).

2) *Altaische Studien* I (*Abhandlungen Berliner Akademie*, 1860, p. 614, note 2). The occasion for this observation is afforded by the Manchu word *abka*, which SCHOTT, on hardly plausible grounds, considers as a corruption of Tib. *namk<sup>c</sup>a*.

3) *J. R. A. S.*, 1909, p. 931, note 3.

4) Compare BUSHELL, *The Early History of Tibet*, p. 7; and F. GRENARD, *Mission scientifique dans la haute Asie*, Vol. II, p. 404 (Paris, 1898). Also the *Tang hiang* 党項, a Tibetan tribe inhabiting the southwestern part of Kan-su and the region of the Kuku-nor, worshipped Heaven with sacrifices of oxen and sheep every three years at a gathering of their clans (三年一聚會殺牛羊以祭天。*Sui shu*, Ch. 83, p. 3). Any Buddhist or Indian influence is here excluded in view of the period in question (589—618).

this word was of Sanskrit origin, is highly improbable. The Chinese account shows us that the Tibetans, in the same manner as the Turkish, Mongol, and other tribes of Asia, in times prior to Indian influence, had a well established worship of Heaven and Earth (as well as of the astral bodies), and this implies the fact that an indigenous word for "heaven" was theirs. This word was *gnam, nam,* or *nam-ka*, and there is no reason, from its phonetic make-up, why it should not plainly be a Tibetan word. The Tibetan lexicographers are very familiar with Sanskrit loan-words, and never fail to point them out in every case; this is not done, however, in the case of the word for "heaven." The archaic form *nam-ka* bears out the fact that *nam* is a good native word, for the suffix *ka* is never attached to a Sanskrit loan-word. [1]) In the same manner as the prefix *g* is noteworthy in *gnam*, so the prefix *m̥* must not be overlooked in the word *m̥kʿa*; the spelling *nam-kʿa* (but frequently enough also *nam-mkʿa*) is a purely graphic expediency, and the outward resemblance to Skr. *kha* is accidental. SCHIEFNER [2]) compared Tib. *m̥kʿa* with Chin. *kʿi* 氣; this equation is untenable chiefly for the reason that Tib. *a* cannot correspond to Chin. *i*, but it shows that Schiefner had sense enough to regard *mkʿa* as a truly Tibetan word. It is widely diffused in the allied languages. [3]) Lolo *mukʿiai* (*ai* = *ä*) [4]) presents a counterpart to Tib. *namkʿa*.

The word *žaṅ lon* occurs three times in the Table. In one passage (IV, 3), M. BACOT takes it in the sense of "minister" and accordingly accepts it as an equivalent of *žaṅ blon*. In III, 5, he translates it "news;" and in XI, 5, we read "indique que l'oncle viendra

1) On the suffix *ka* (*kʿa, ga*) see SCHIEFNER, *Mélanges asiatiques*, Vol. I, p. 380.

2) *L. c.*, p. 340.

3) Compare the list of words for "heaven" in Mission D'OLLONE, *Langues des peuples non chinois de la Chine*, p. 24, Paris, 1912, particularly such forms as *hé ka, mu ko, m'keuk, nakamu, mongkele*.

4) P. VIAL, *Dictionnaire français-lolo*, p. 88 (Hongkong, 1909).

aux nouvelles," where the text offers *bdag žaṅ lon-du oṅ-bar ston.* In the latter case, M. BACOT separates the compound, and assumes *žaṅ-(po)* = maternal uncle, and *lon* = tidings, message; but this is not very possible. Further, the word *bdag* [1]) must not be overlooked in this sentence, and *oṅ-ba* in connection with the terminative means "to become;" so that I think the sense of the sentence is, "It indicates that I shall become a *žaṅ lon.*" It goes without saying that in the three passages this word is one and the same, and can but have the same significance. The word *lon,* accordingly, is written without the prefix *b.* This way of writing cannot be considered an anomaly, but exactly corresponds to the pronunciation of the word at that period, as we established on the basis of the transcription *lun* 論 (= Tib. *blon*) furnished by the Annals of the T$^{c}$ang Dynasty (*Kiu T$^{c}$ang shu,* Ch. 196 上, p. 1; *T$^{c}$ang shu,* Ch. 216 上, p. 1) and the inscription of 822. The word *btsan,* the title of the kings of Tibet, was likewise sounded *tsan,* as evidenced by the Chinese transcription *tsan* 贊. [2]) The prefixed media

1) The word *bdag,* the personal pronoun of the first person, occurs several times in the answers of the Table (VII, 1; VIII, 7, 8; XI, 7). In this connection it should be remembered that *bdag sgrog,* "crying *bdag,*" is one of the synonyms of the raven (given in the Dictionary of the French Missionaries, p. 86); it is evidently an imitation of Skr. *ātmaghosha,* a synonym of the crow, which is rendered in the Tibetan version of *Amarakosha* (ed. *Bibl. ind.,* p. 184) *sgrogs-pai bdag-ñid-can.*

2) It has been asserted that the Chinese term *tsan-p$^{c}$u* 贊普 corresponds to Tibetan *btsan-po* (BUSHELL, *The Early History of Tibet,* p. 104, note *a*; CHAVANNES, *Documents,* pp. 150, 186). But this identification is not exact; the Chinese words very accurately reproduce the Tibetan form *(b)tsan-p$^{c}$o,* as is evidenced first by the presence of the labial aspirate in the Chinese word *p$^{c}$u,* and secondly by the gloss expressly given in *T$^{c}$ang shu* (Ch. 216 上, p. 1): 丈夫曰普 "a man is called in Tibetan *p$^{c}$u.*" This explanation leaves no doubt that the Tibetan noun *p$^{c}$o* "man," and not the mere suffix *po,* is intended, which, by the way, is transcribed in Chinese *pu* 逋, as shown by many examples in *T$^{c}$ang shu*; for instance, in the titles of the ministers, as *nang lun ch$^{c}$ö pu* 囊論掣逋 = Tib. *naṅ blon c$^{c}$e-po,* "great minister of the interior." This reading *(b)tsan-p$^{c}$o* is confirmed by a Lhasa inscription of the ninth century published by Mr. WADDELL (*J. R. A. S.,* 1909, pp. 1269, 1280), where the word is written twice *btsan-p$^{c}$o*; it

*b*, accordingly, is not an integral part of these two stems, but an additional prefix which must have a grammatical function; and this, in my opinion, is that it forms *nomina actionis*, in a similar manner as it designates a past action in connection with verbal roots. The stem *tsan* means "powerful, warlike, heroic;" *b-tsan*, "one having the title or dignity of *tsan*"; *b-lon*, "one who has the function of, or acts as, minister." What is a *žaṅ lon*? 1) Mr. WADDELL (*J. R. A. S.*, 1909, p. 1274) explains that this term means "uncle-minister," and designates "a sort of privy councillor, a title previously borne apparently only by the highest ministers, some or

---

certainly does not mean, as alleged by Mr. WADDELL, "the mighty father" (father is *p'a*; *p'o* never means "father," but only "male, man"), but "the martial man," "the male hero" (*tsan*, as *T'ang shu* says, means *kiang hiung* 疆雄). The stress laid on the word "male" is very natural; as there always were, and still are, also queens ruling Tibetan tribes (compare the account of the Tibetan Women's Kingdom in *Sui shu*, Ch. 83). The contrast is clearly enough expressed in the *T'ang shu*, which adds, "The wife of the Tsan-p'u is called *mo mung* 末蒙." Whatever the latter element may represent, it is evident that the first is the Tibetan word *mo*, "woman." (A royal consort is called in Tibetan *lcam-mo*, *btsun-mo*, or *a'uṅ-ma*; probably the Chinese *mo-mung* represents an ancient Tibetan word still unknown to us, which would be *mo-moṅ*; Chinese *mung* phonetically corresponds to Tib. *moṅ*, as proved by *Hua i yi yü* [Ch. 18, p. 65], where Tib. *rṅa-moṅ* ["camel"] is transliterated in Chinese 兒阿蒙; in *rGyal rabs* [fol. 79] one of the wives of King Sroṅ-btsan is styled *Moṅ bza k'ri lcam*, which indeed goes to prove that a word *moṅ* in the sense of "royal consort" must have existed in ancient Tibetan.) The king is therefore styled the "male warrior" in opposition to the attribute "female" appearing in the title of his queen. The inscription of 822 (see the facsimile in BUSHELL's paper, pl. II, line 2) writes the word *btsan-po*; WADDELL sets the date of his inscription on inward evidence in 842—4; so that it must be granted that both ways of writing co-existed at that period. The writing *btsan-p'o* doubtless is the older one, and appears as the index of the ancient matriarchal conditions of Tibet at a stage when masculine power gradually emerged from the institution of female preponderance. When the sway of the Central Tibetan kings was ultimately established in the male line of succession, the plain *btsan-po*, without emphasis of sex, was allowed to take its permanent place. Note that according to *T'ang shu* (BUSHELL, *l. c.*, p. 98) the inhabitants of the Women's Kingdom elected a man as their ruler from 742.

1) JÄSCHKE (*Dictionary*, p. 471) quotes the word from *rGyal rabs*, saying that it seems to be a kind of title given to a minister (or magistrate); wisely enough, he makes it a separate heading, and does not link it with the word *žaṅ-po*, "uncle." So do also the French Missionaries (p. 845).

most of whom were of the blood-royal." This is a surmise which is not founded on any evidence.

The Tibetan administrative system is entirely based on Chinese institutions; and the official style of the Tibetan chancery, as clearly demonstrated by the Tibetan inscriptions of the Tᶜang period, is modelled on that of China.[1]) For the explanation of Tibetan terms relating to officialdom, we have in the majority of cases to look to China. What a *žaṅ lon* is, is plainly stated in *Tᶜang shu* (*l. c.*), where we meet it in the garb *shang lun* 尙論. The nine Tibetan

1) A feature to which Mr. WADDELL in his *Lhasa Edicts*, and Mr. A. H. FRANCKE in his rendering of the inscription of 822, did not pay attention, wherefore they missed the meaning of several phrases which cannot be derived from a literal translation of the Tibetan words in their ordinary sense, but which must be viewed through Chinese spectacles, and taken as imitations of Chinese documentary and epigraphical style. But this subject calls for a special investigation. To this Chinese official terminology belongs, for example, the Tibetan designation of the people as "black-headed" (*mgo nag*), which is purely and simply copied from Chinese phraseology, as it is likewise when it occurs in the Orkhon inscriptions and among the Mongols. Mr. WADDELL (*J. R. A. S.*, 1909, p. 1255) remarks on this term that it "probably may denote that in those days the Tibetans did not wear caps; indeed, the caps at the present day are all of Chinese pattern and manufactured in China." In this case, Mr. WADDELL must unfortunately forego the claim to originality, for the present writer was the first to advance this explanation, but with reference to ancient China (*Tᶜoung Pao*, 1908, p. 40), and supported it also with good reasons based on the peculiar ceremonial character of Chinese head-gear. With regard to Tibet, however, this interpretation is out of place. There, it is plainly a loan-word, an artificial imitation of Chinese official speech. Further, Mr. WADDELL's observation that all Tibetan caps are of Chinese pattern and manufacture is erroneous, as a glance at ROCKHILL's *Notes on the Ethnology of Tibet* (pp. 688—689, *Report U. S. Nat. Mus.*, 1893) and his plates 3—4 will convince one. The Tibetan nomads living on the high and cold plateaus naturally always wore fur caps and manufactured them themselves, and there is a large variety of types of indigenous head-gear, without Chinese affinities, everywhere in eastern Tibet and in the Kukunor region (so also F. GRENARD, *Mission scient. dans la haute Asie*, Vol. II, p. 340, Paris, 1898); even the round felt caps made in Peking for the Mongol and Tibetan market do not at all represent a Chinese but a Mongol-Tibetan style of cap. As in so many other cases, the Chinese have taken into their hands an industry of their subjected neighbors, and cater to their taste. Tibetan officials certainly wear the caps of the Chinese official costume made in, and imported from, China, but that is all. And the manifold styles of priestly head-gear, partially like the *paṇ žva* traced to Indian traditions, certainly do not come from China.

Boards of Ministry are there enumerated, which it is said are designated with the general name 尙論掣逋突瞿 *shang lun ch'ö pu t'u kiü* (**du gu*), which, as stated, may be taken as transcription of Tibetan *žaṅ* (*b*)*lon c'e-po dgu*, "the Nine Great Boards." The word *žaṅ* cannot be explained through Tibetan, and indeed is nothing but the Tibetan transcription of Chinese *shang* 尙; and *ˌžaṅ* (*b*)*lon*, "chief minister," corresponds in meaning to *shang shu* 尙書, "President of a Board," a term rendered in the inscription (above, No. 20) by Tib. *c'en-po*. Tib. *žaṅ* is a strictly phonetic transcription of 尙, as both agree in tone, *shang*[4] having the sinking lower tone, and *žaṅ* being low-toned; the Tibetans cannot write Chinese *shang*[4] with the voiceless palatal sibilant *š*, as all words with this initial sound have the high tone, but for this reason must resort to the deep-toned *ž*.[1]) The tone, as pointed out before, is a matter

1) In the Tibetan vocabulary contained in Ch. 11 of *Hua i yi yü* (Hirth's copy in the Royal Library of Berlin), the Tibetan words are all transliterated in Chinese characters according to their Tibetan spelling (the transliterations do not reproduce the Tibetan pronunciation), and the rule is usually observed to transcribe a Tibetan word with initial *ž* by means of a Chinese syllable in the lower tone; for example, Tib. *žiṅ* to be read *shêng* 繩, Tib. *žag* to be read *hia* 厦, Tib. *žu* to be read *jo* 㸐 or *shu* 熟. If Tib. *šu* renders Chin. *shui* 水 in the inscription of 822 (see above, p. 79), this exception is only seeming, and confirms the rule; for *shui* has the rising upper tone, consequently the Tibetans rendered it with *šu* in the high tone, being their tone nearest to the Chinese, while Tib. *žu* has the deep tone. *Vice versa*, Chinese *š* is transcribed by the Tibetans *ž*, for example, *shêng* 省 "province" being transcribed Tib. *žiṅ* in *Shambhalai lam yig* (regarding this work compare *T'oung Pao*, 1907, p. 403), and Tib. *š* is transcribed by Chin. *ž*, for instance, Tib. *šo* = 若 *žo* at the end of royal names, occurring in three names of King *Sroṅ btsan*'s ancestors (*T'ang shu*, Ch. 216 上, p. 2 a): 揭利失若 *Kie* (**kut*, Korean *kal*) *li ši*(*t*) *žo* = Tib. *Gal* (?) *ri* ("mountain") *žid* (?) *šo*; 勃弄若 *P'o lung žo* = Tib. *P'o sroṅ šo*; and 詎素若 *Kü* (**gio, gu*) *so*(*k*) *žo* = Tib. *Go* (?) *sug* (?) *šo*. There is no doubt of the identification of Chin. *žo* with Tib. *šo*, as this Tibetan word is indeed found with four of the so-called "six terrestrial *Legs*" (*sa-i legs drug*): *ˌO šo*, *De šo*, *T'i šo*; *ˌI šo* (*dPag bsam ljon bzaṅ*, p. 150, l. 12). Then we have allied words in both languages: as Tib. *ša*, "flesh, meat" = Chin. *žou* (*jou*) 肉; Tib. *šes*, "knowledge, to know" = Chin. *či* 知 and 智; Tib (*b*)*cu*, "ten" = Chin. *ši*

of importance in the study of Tibeto-Chinese and Chinese-Tibetan transcriptions. The fact that Tibetan *žaṅ* really corresponds to Chinese 尙 is evidenced by the inscription of 822, where the word *žaṅ* in the titles of the Tibetan ministers repeatedly occurs, being rendered in each case by Chin. *shang* (above, Nos. 9, 10, 13, 15, 19). It is therefore beyond any doubt that the equation Tib. *žaṅ* = Chin. *shang* 尙 belonged to the permanent equipment of the Tibeto-Chinese chancery in the first part of the ninth century. [1])

The most interesting phonetic phenomenon of our text is the writing *dmyig* for *mig*, "eye." There cannot be any doubt of this identification, as the word is required by the context, as it is determined by the adjective *rno*, "sharp," and the phrase *dmyig rno* is a parallelism to the following *sñan gsan*, "to have a sharp ear."

---

十; Tib. *lce*, "tongue" = Chin. *šé* 舌. The words *žo*, "milk" = Chin. *žu* 乳, and *šig*, "louse" = Chin. *ši(t)* 虱, seem to belong to an earlier stage of relationship between the two languages.

1) The word *shang* appears as the first element in the names of three Tibetan generals who attacked China in 765 (*Kiu T'ang shu*, Ch. 196 上, p. 10 a; BUSHELL, *The Early History of Tibet*, p. 45): *Shang kie si tsan mo* 尙結息贊磨, who died in 797; *Shang si tung tsan* 尙息東贊 (Tib. *Žaṅ ston btsan*); and *Shang ye si* 尙野息 (a fourth is called *Ma chung ying* 馬重英). Under the year 768 (*ibid.*, Ch. 196 下, p. 1) a general *Shang si mo* 尙悉摩 (BUSHELL, p. 48: *Shang tsan mo*) is mentioned. *T'ang shu* (Ch. 216 下, p. 6 b) has a Tibetan commander-in-chief *Shang t'a tsang* 尙塔藏 (Tib. *Žaṅ t'a? bzaṅ*). In these cases Chin. *shang* corresponds to Tib. *žaṅ*, which is a well-known clan name based on the district of this name in the province of *gTsaṅ* (CHANDRA DAS, *Dictionary*, p. 1065). One of the ministers of King *K'ri-sroṅ* was *Žaṅ ñams bzaṅ* (*dPag bsam ljon bzaṅ*, p. 170); in *rGyal rabs* we meet a minister *Žaṅ dbu riṅ* and the well-known translator *Bandhe Ye-šes sde* with the clan name *Žaṅ sna-nam*, that is, from *Sna-nam* in *Žaṅ* (CHANDRA DAS, p. 765, is wrong to refer in this case to Samarkand; as a clan name *Sna-nam* relates to a place in the district *Žaṅ* in the province *gTsaṅ*). — In the iconographical work "The Three Hundred Gods of Narthang" (section *Rin ḥbyuṅ*, fols. 112, 113) a deity is represented in three forms under the name *Žaṅ blon rdo-rje bdud ḥdul*. *rDo-rje bdud ḥdul* (with the title and office of *žaṅ blon*), "the Subduer of Māra by means of the Vajra," appears as a sorcerer at the time of K'ri-sroṅ lde-btsan (*Roman*, p. 122). — Also the T'u-yü-hun had the office of *shang shu* (*Sui shu*, Ch. 83, p. 1 b).

Also the Lama bsTan-pa du-ldan (p. 448, line 3) has perfectly understood the word in the sense of *mig*. The spelling *dmyig* is neither erroneous nor arbitrary, but proves that at the time when, and in the locality where, our text was written, the word was actually articulated *dmyig*, as here spelled; for in the dialect of the Jyarung, [1]) inhabiting the northwestern part of the present Chinese province of Sze-chᶜuan, I actually heard the word articulated *dmye*. The form *dmig* is still found in modern popular texts; for instance, twice in the small work *Sa bdag klu gñan-gyi byad grol*, along with the orthography *mig* four times (*Ein Sühngedicht der Bonpo*, *l. c.*, p. 21). It is therefore patent how important it is to observe carefully such

1) The Jyarung styled Kin-ch'uan 金川 by the Chinese (see M. Jametel, *L'épigraphie chinoise au Tibet*, p. 31, Paris, 1880) are a group of Tibetan tribes inhabiting the high mountain-valleys of Sze-ch'uan Province. The name is written in Tibetan *rgya-roṅ* which is explained as "Chinese ravines." Of their language we possess only scant vocabularies. B. Hodgson (*Essays on the Languages*, etc., *of Nepal and Tibet*, pp. 65—82, London, 1874) offers a vocabulary of 176 words. T. de Lacouperie (*Les langues de la Chine avant les Chinois*, pp. 78—80, Paris, 1888) has some remarks on the language. A. v. Rosthorn has published a vocabulary in a volume of *Z. D. M. G.* (owing to a misplacement of my notes referring to it, I regret being unable for the present to give an exact reference). Jyarung is one of the most archaic Tibetan dialects in which not only the ancient prefixes are still articulated (*rgyal* "king," *stoṅ* "thousand," *šta* "horse"), but also single and even double prefixes appear where literary Tibetan has none at all; they are supermen in prefixes, or, if it is permissible to coin the word, superprefixists. They say, for example, *drmi* for common Tib. *mi*, "man"; the prefix *d* largely enters the names for the organs of the body; as *dmye* "eye," *dešnä* (*sna*) "nose," *desü'e* (*so*) "tooth," *drnä'* (*rna*) "ear," *dešmi'* (*lce*) "tongue," *demjä'* "chin," *demki'* (*ske*) "neck." This corroborates my opinion that the prefixes are survivals of ancient numeratives; for this reason they are not stable, but variable, in the various dialects. The Jyarung language not only had numeratives different from standard Tibetan, but also arranged its words under different categories, so that they appear with prefixes entirely at variance with other dialects: thus, *tayák*, "hand" (*p'yag*), *poṅi'*, "silver" (*dṅul*). The stems, accordingly, are *ṅi*, *ṅul* (Hakka *ṅ'iu*, Burmese *ṅwe*), *po* and *d* being prefixes. The Jyarung numerals are 1 *ktig* or *kti'*, 2 *knis*, 3 *ksam*, 4 *kbli*, 5 *kmu*, 6 *kčo*, 7 *kšnis*, 8 *vryad*, 9 *kṅu*, 10 *šči*. The numerals 4—7 and 9, at variance with standard Tibetan, have been raised into the *k*- category in analogy with 1—3, which agree with standard Tibetan. It is of especial interest that in the numeral 3, *ksam*, Jyarung agrees in the *a* vowel with Chinese *sam* where standard Tibetan has *u* (*gsum*), and that in the numeral 5, *kṅu*, Jyarung agrees in the *u* vowel with Chinese *ṅu* where standard Tibetan has *a* (*lṅa*).

variations of spelling, even in recent manuscripts and prints, and it is obvious also that they cannot always be laid down as clerical errors. This has likewise a bearing upon ancient manuscripts; the mere occurrence of abnormal, obsolete, or dialectic forms is not sufficient evidence for pronouncing the verdict that the said manuscript or work is old, while certainly the total evidence presented by archaisms will always influence our judgment in favor of a greater antiquity. It would be, for example, perfectly conceivable to me that a Jyarung Lama who, owing to the far-reaching divergence of his tongue from the written language, is forced to study the latter thoroughly, as we, for instance, would study Latin, will be inclined to write the word *mig* in the form *dmyig* or *dmig*. Analogous to the latter is the form *dmag-pa* (Table XI, 1) for the more common *mag-pa*; and as the prefix *d* before *m*, in cases where the written language is without a prefix, is a characteristic of the Jyarung dialect, the conclusion may be hazarded that the *document Pelliot* was composed either in a locality where a dialect identical with, or allied to, Jyarung was spoken, or that, regardless of the locality where the composition took place, the author of the document was conversant with a language related in phonology to Jyarung.

What is the meaning of the prefixed dental *d*? In the written language we find such formations as *ma*, "below," — *dma*, "to be low;" *maṅ*, "many," — *dmaṅs*, "multitude," and *dmag*, "army;" *mig*, "eye," — *dmig*, "hole." The formations with the prefix *d* apparently are secondary derivatives from the stem beginning with *m*. Comparison with the allied languages tends to confirm this opinion; *mig* is the Tibetan stem-word, as shown by Lepcha *a-mik*, Burmese *myak* (*myet*), Kuki-Chin *mit*, *mi(k)*, [1] Chinese *muk* 目. In all Indo-Chinese languages we observe that nouns are clas-

1) Sten Konow, *Z. D. M. G.*, Vol. LVI, 1902, p. 506.

sified into certain categories, and that each of these categories is associated with a particular numerative. The numerative is the index or outward symbol of the mental association underlying these categories of ideas. These numeratives, with a few exceptions, have disappeared from modern Tibetan, but they are preserved in many of the so-called prefixes which represent their survivals, and this is the usual function of prefixes in nouns (though they certainly have also other origins and functions). The original significance of the majority of them can no longer be made out, and will probably remain obscure; the numerous variations of prefixes in the dialects indicate that there has been a large number of differing numeratives from remote times. A few examples may serve as illustration. The prefix *m* appears in connection with words denoting organs of the body, and it is curious that there are groups with the same initial sounds. There is a *mc*$^c$ group, — *mc*$^c$*ed* "body," *mc*$^c$*e-ba* "tusk," *mc*$^c$*er-pa* "spleen," *mc*$^c$*in-pa* "liver," *mc*$^c$*an* "side of the breast," *mc*$^c$*u* "lip," *mc*$^c$*i-ma* "tear," *mc*$^c$*il-ma* "spittle;" there is a *mg* group, — *mgo* "head," *mgur*, *mgul* "throat," *mgrin-pa* "neck," a *mk*$^c$ group, — *mk*$^c$*al-ma* "kidneys," *mk*$^c$*ris-pa* "bile," *mk*$^c$*rig-ma* "wrist," *mk*$^c$*ur-ba* "cheek." The occurrence of the prefix *m* in these fifteen words belonging to the same category of idea cannot be accidental, and the supposition of a former numerative *m* joined to names of bodily parts seems a plausible explanation for its presence. The following groups are also suggestive: *ldad-pa* "to chew," *ldan-pa* "cheek," and *ldag-pa*, "to lick;" *lte-ba* "navel," *lto-ba* "stomach," and *ltogs-pa* "hunger;" *rkaṅ-pa* "foot," *rke* "waist," *rkan* "palate," *rkub* "anus."

The laws of *sandhi*, as established by the Tibetan grammarians,[1])

---

1) The generally adopted metrical versions are given in text and translation in *Studien zur Sprachwissenschaft der Tibeter* (*Sitzungsberichte der bayerischen Akademie*, 1898, pp. 579—587).

are not strictly observed. The indefinite article *žig* is correctly employed after nouns ending in a vowel, *n* and *m*: *dgra žig, gñen žig, mye ṅan žig, gtam žig; rton cig* in. V. 23 is correct owing to the existing *da drug*; [1]) *cig* correctly in *myi rgod cig; ri-dags žig* instead of *šig*. Of designations of the genitive, we find *-i, kyi,* and *gi*, but not *gyi*: *lhai, pʻyogs-kyi, bud-myed-kyi, dguṅ-gi*; but *yul-gi, žaṅ-lon-gi*, instead of *gyi*; likewise in the instrumental case, *gñen-gis, gcan-zan-gis*. The termination of the terminative is *du*: *žaṅ-lon-du, ạbriṅ-du, pʻyag du* (instead of *tu*), *mtʻo du* (V. 19) instead of *mtʻo-ru* or *mtʻor*, but *dgu-r* (V. 11), *bzaṅ-por* (V. 25), *riṅs-par* (V. 27); also *ltas-su* (V. 12) is a regular formation. The suffix *tu* after vowels occurs in modern manuscripts likewise. [2]) The particle *te* of the gerund, with its variants, is utilized according to rule: *kʻyer-te, kʻrid-de, rñed-de, ši-ste.*

---

1) Compare the rule as formulated in *Za-ma-tog, l. c.*, p. 584; and above, p. 61, note 2.

2) *Ein Sühngedicht der Bonpo, l. c.*, p. 22.

Additional Notes. — Regarding the crow of orientation employed by the navigators (p. 11, note), see now also R. Otto Franke (*Dīghanikāya*, p. 166, Göttingen, 1913). Franke claims for himself the priority in having established the fact of this practice of mariners; but Minayev, at any rate, was the first to explain correctly the term *disākāka*.

On p. 29, after line 21, the following was omitted through an oversight of the printer: In *K.* we meet the sentence *tʻag riṅs-su ạgro-bar ạgyur-ro*, "you will set out on a distant journey;" the same is expressed in the Table in genuinely popular style by *lam riṅ-por dgos-pa.*

Note on p. 95. In regard to Tʻu-po see also Hirth, *Sinologische Beiträge zur Geschichte der Türk-Völker* (*Bull. Ac. St.-Pét.*, 1900, p. 242). The sole object of the note above referred to was to discuss the relation of the Chinese to the Tibetan and alleged Tibetan names.